LEAVING HOME

LEAVING HOME

Gill Jones

OPEN UNIVERSITY PRESS
Buckingham · Philadelphia

Open University Press
Celtic Court
22 Ballmoor
Buckingham
MK18 1XW

and
1900 Frost Road, Suite 101
Bristol, PA 19007, USA

First Published 1995

A catalogue record of this book is available from the British Library

ISBN   0–335–19284–X (pb)   0–335–19285–8 (hb)

Library of Congress Cataloging-in-Publication Data
Jones, Gill, 1942–
    Leaving home / Gill Jones.
        p.   cm.
    Includes bibliographical references and index.
    ISBN 0–335–19285–8 (hb.) – ISBN 0–335–19284–X (pbk.)
    1. Young adults—Great Britain—Social conditions.   2. Young
adults—Housing—Great Britain.   3. Youth—Great Britain—Social
conditions.   4. Youth—Housing—Great Britain.   5. Home—Great
Britain.   I. Title.
HQ799.8.G7J65   1995
305.23′5′0941–dc20   94–41292
                                                                                    CIP

Typeset by Graphicraft Typesetters Limited, Hong Kong
Printed in Great Britain by Biddles Limited, Guildford and Kings Lynn

To the memory of my parents,
Arnold and Betty Jones

Contents

List of figures
and tables

Preface

This book has been in preparation for a long time. I imagine that many social scientists research issues which touch them personally. Since the mingling of autobiography with scientific enquiry seems increasingly acceptable, I am encouraged to identify, briefly, how the research issue of leaving home relates to and is also informed by my own personal and professional biography.

My professional interest stems from my experience as a social worker in Inner London, when I worked with young people and their families. They often sought social work help because they could no longer live together. Young people wanted to leave home. Sometimes their parents wanted them away from home. Various 'solutions' were worked out, but it seemed that for a section of the population, at least, leaving home was quite a traumatic event. How, I wondered, did other young people leave home?

My personal experience has also been influential. I left home to go to university when I was 19 years of age, and never returned to live with my parents. I did not know when I left that I was leaving for good, and the myth that I had not was perpetuated by my parents virtually until their deaths in 1989. They always called their home my home. The definition and location of 'home' was complex for me as well, as I was living in what is technically known as a single-person household. Was my home the place where I lived, or the family home where my parents lived? Or even something less tangible, relating to my homeland, the area where I was born and spent my childhood, but which I left much earlier?

When I left social work and began social science research in 1982, I discovered that there was in fact very little research on leaving home in Britain, and that I could obtain access to survey data which would allow me to fill a part of the gap. There was clearly a need for more general research on national patterns and variations. And my personal experience had revealed the problem of definitions and indicated the need for a theoretically sound understanding. Within the main thrust of my work on transitions and inequalities in youth, it is a research area to which I have kept returning.

Since this book is based on a programme of research over more than a decade, I am indebted to a lot of organizations and people without whose support, advice and help it would not have been possible. The debt extends from my PhD supervisors, Nigel Gilbert and Sara Arber at Surrey University, to my current colleagues, Andrew McPherson and David Raffe at the Centre for Educational Sociology (CES), University of Edinburgh. The first two put me on the path and the second two made it possible for me to progress along it. The data on which this book is based comes mainly from the Scottish Young People's Survey, which was funded by the Scottish Office Education Department, the Industry Department for Scotland, the Training Agency and the Department of Employment, and conducted by the CES Survey Team. In the course of my work at CES, I have had considerable encouragement from colleagues in Edinburgh, and derived immeasurable benefit from the infrastructure of support for research which, as an Economic and Social Research Council Research Centre, the CES provides.

A large part of this book draws on a two-year research project, 'Young people in and out of the housing market', supported by the Joseph Rowntree Foundation. The project was jointly run with the Scottish Council for Single Homeless (SCSH). I am therefore indebted to the Joseph Rowntree Foundation; to Laurie Naumann, and subsequently Claire Stevens, who were involved in the project in their roles as Directors of SCSH; to members of the project advisory committee for their advice and support; to Linda Gilliland who conducted all the in-depth interviews with sensitivity, and without whose work the qualitative case study material presented here would not exist; and to Alison Mason who transcribed the tapes and made it possible for the richness of the original language to be retained. I am grateful to Joan Hughes for checking the final manuscript and to all those who commented on earlier drafts and working papers, including Bob Coles, Radiance Strathdee, Isabel Anderson, Lynn Jamieson and David Raffe. The major thanks go, however, to the thousands of young people who, by giving up their time to fill in questionnaires and be interviewed, provided the data. The views expressed in this book are mine alone.

Gill Jones
Edinburgh

List of abbreviations

CEC	Commission of the European Communities
CES	Centre for Educational Sociology
DSS	Department of Social Security
ESRC	Economic and Social Research Council
EU	European Union
GHS	General Household Survey
IS	Income Support
NCDS	National Child Development Study
OPCS	Office of Population Censuses and Surveys
SCSH	Scottish Council for Single Homeless
SSAC	Social Security Advisory Committee
SYPS	Scottish Young People's Survey

Chapter 1
The construction of a social problem

Leaving the parental home is a normal part of the overall process of transition from dependent childhood to independent citizenship. It is generally expected that as young people grow up, they will move away from the home in which they were raised and eventually establish homes of their own, in which to raise a new generation of children. The move away from the family home is linked with other strands in the transition to adult citizenship, in particular the transition through education and training into the labour market, and the formation of a new family.

Industrial and postindustrial societies lack the distinct rites of passage which mark the attainment of adulthood in many non-industrial societies, and so there is no 'moment' when adulthood can be celebrated. Though the legal age of majority is 18 years, many of the rights and responsibilities associated with adult independence in modern Britain are conferred at other ages, and youth emerges as a extended period in which a gradual transition is effected between childhood and citizenship, mediated by the family and the state (Jones and Wallace 1992). Leaving home for the first time is one of several important events in this transition and it is an event which most of us have experienced. It is possible that, compared with other transition events such as leaving school, starting one's first job, forming a partnership or having a baby, leaving home may be gaining in significance (Harris 1983).

It seems, though, that the normality of leaving home and its function in the transition to adulthood is becoming lost from view. The increased incidence of homelessness in youth is one contributory factor. Concerns about an apparent breakdown of family life are another. As a result, objectivity and conceptual clarity are lost. Now, in the mid-1990s, there is more talk about preventing young people from leaving home than celebrating it as a major event in the transition to adulthood. Leaving home is seen as inherently problematic. It is important to do some unpacking of the issue, removing moral and emotional overtones, and thus to restore clarity to its study. The outcomes of leaving home – housing and homelessness – should be disentangled from the process of leaving home itself. Only then can we understand any problems young people may have when they leave home and try to enter the housing market, and find appropriate solutions where these are needed. And appropriate interventions *are* needed if youth homelessness is not to be seen in the next millennium as one of the most shameful products of late twentieth-century society.

This book examines the process of leaving home and the problems many young people face on trying to enter the housing market, locating homelessness at one end of a continuum of risk. This approach allows us to consider the extent to which housing risk is shared, and the extent to which it can be avoided. The recent research on which much of the book is based was designed specifically towards this aim. Findings from national surveys have been combined with findings from a survey of homeless young people, and qualitative interviews, so that the risks associated with leaving home can be explored, and homelessness seen in context. In this way, we can also learn a great deal more about leaving home.

Home and homelessness

The first 'unpacking' task concerns the concept of 'home'. Leaving home is a fusion of two transitions: to independent housing and to an independent household (the latter linked perhaps with family formation). This fusion leads to *con*fusion, as 'leaving home' means leaving a family as well as leaving an address. 'Homelessness' similarly confounds two issues: lack of housing and lack of co-domiciled family. These points relate to definitions of 'home'. The title of this book, *Leaving Home*, is therefore potentially dangerously simplistic. The expression is neither as simple as it sounds, nor as 'problematic' as its constructions.

The concept of 'home', whatever its reality, is overlaid with the domestic idyll, and family relationships are so central to ideas about home life (Allan and Crow 1989) that home and family are virtually interchangeable terms (Oakley 1976), and a home is only a home as long as the family is in it – otherwise it is 'only a house' (Gilman 1980). Indeed, Leonard (1980) suggested that 'to set up home alone or with peers is a contradiction in folk terms'. Households which do not conform to the normative image (nuclear family households) can be regarded as deviant. The term 'leaving home' can thus imply a loss of family, and even a form of family breakdown. Single-person or peer households, to which many young people move when they leave home, are therefore also problematic.

'Home' is thus not just about housing, but also about a household, and preferably a family household. Underlying the domestic idyll is an often uncomfortable reality. The home is more likely to fulfil the needs of the head of household, who is usually male (and whose 'home is his castle'), than those of other family members, as Allan and Crow (1989) indicate. Some commentators have pointed out that for many women, home can be a prison (Graham 1983); others similarly suggest that for the unemployed, life can be home-centred in a negative, retreatist way (Binns and Mars 1984), while elderly people may be 'homebound' (Deem 1985). The concept of home as 'sanctuary' or 'place of secure retreat' (Moore 1984) does not necessarily hold true for those in weaker positions in the domestic power relationships, including young people.

The 'home' is the locus of inequality between parents and children, just as it is the locus of gender inequality between husband and wife. Young people's emancipation from parental control – an essential part of the transition to adulthood in western industrialized societies – therefore involves moving out of the home of their parents and establishing a home of their own, for which they have responsibility and in which they have power and control. The parental home 'belongs' to the household head, even though young people may still refer to it as theirs (Ainley's 1991 research found that young people who reported living in 'their own homes' were often living with their parents). Nevertheless, young people (over 18 years of age in England and Wales, but over 16 in Scotland) can only live in the parental home as licensees of their parents (i.e. with permission). In this sense, it is the parental home and not the family home. Family members may not all have the right to live there.

Not all young people would consider home as a domestic idyll. Some have experienced unhappiness there, and some have experienced abuse. Others have been removed from home in childhood, and have lived in alternative 'surrogate' family settings, in foster homes or care institutions. For all of these, 'home' – and the extent to which the concept involves family life – may have very different connotations. Some of those living in unhappy family homes or local authority care may consider themselves already homeless.

Somerville (1992) comments on a distinction between home as an ideal and home as a reality, and argues that the social construction of 'home' – and homelessness – involves both. Watson and Austerberry (1986) define different dimensions in the construction of concepts of home and homelessness which combine housing and household elements: material conditions, emotional and physical well-being, loving and caring social relations, control and privacy, and living/sleeping space. Their research indicated that the inconsistent use of different elements in the social construction of 'home' and 'homeless' leads to confusion about whether people are homeless or not. The extent to which social relations are inherent in the understanding of 'home', and lack of social relations in the concept of 'homeless', remains very problematic. Homeless young people, as we shall see, place stress on having a family as well as being housed. Their constructions of 'home' are therefore normative. Though more people are living in single-person households, the image of 'home' does not therefore conform to the changing reality.

It is important to distinguish between the housing and household elements which make up the concepts of home and homelessness. The action of *leaving* home takes place at the junction between the public and private worlds, and involves leaving people as well as a building. It may also involve leaving a community. Similarly, *setting up* home involves entry into the housing market and the formation of a household. Young people standing on the threshold between living as a child in their family home and moving out to an independent home face contradictory pressures, urging them across the threshold or urging them to stay.

The 'problem' of leaving home

Leaving home lends itself easily to misconstructions because the act of leaving home is associated at many levels with some quite intense emotions. For the young person leaving home, it may be a step from known security into unknown risk, combining excitement with fear. For the parent, it may mark the successful achievement of their parenting function, but at the same time the onset of the mid-life stage and loss of one of their main social roles. It may be as difficult for parents to cope with the departure of their children, the resulting 'empty nest' (as demographers refer to it), as it is for young people to manage on their own. And finally, by leaving home and seeking to take their place in society as emancipated adults, young people are trying to enter into a social contract with the state. As dependent children it was their parents who held this contract on their behalf. By leaving home, they are effectively acknowledging the responsibilities and claiming the rights of adult citizens. Many of them are doing this at a time when society has very little to offer them (with widespread unemployment, a shortage of affordable housing and a withdrawal of the safety net of state social security), and the embarrassment about what to do about young people's demands for a role in society turns into fear of the younger generation. Much of the current government policy directed at young people is concerned with privatizing their care and control onto their families, and blaming parents when they are deemed to have failed. When young people are living at home, their parents act as an interface between them and the outside world, protecting each side from the other. When young people leave home, this interface is withdrawn.

The result, particularly evident in the last few years, has been 'moral panics' surrounding young people and family life, and associated policy attempts emanating from the New Right to deal with the problem of youth homelessness and other problems in youth by extending and increasing the responsibilities of their parents.

'The youth problem'

As a society we appear to have little understanding of the problems young people face as they try to become independent and full citizens. This is evident in government policies affecting young people in Britain, from newspaper coverage of stories relating to young people, and from the paranoia which occasionally arises about moral decline, youth crime, teenage pregnancy and so on. The focus tends to be on the problems young people appear to pose for society, rather than on the problems society creates for the young. In a world in which increased individual choice and consumer rights are stressed, the choices and rights of young people are ignored. After all, rights and choice are the rewards good citizens gain in recognition of their contribution to society, and young people therefore do not deserve rights on this account. That, at least, is the argument. Two issues at least are ignored in its making: that young people's opportunities to contribute to society are limited by the social structure itself; and that young people do indeed contribute a great deal, but their contributions tend to be in the private and unseen world of family life, rather than in the public arena, and so they are ignored.

The responsibilities of society, on the other hand, are not so much ignored as rejected by those in power in present-day Britain. Thus, the differential ability of young people, or the unemployed, or the elderly, or those with disabilities, to contribute to society tends not to be seen as a structural inequality which could be adjusted through state intervention, but as a failure at a personal level. Charles Murray has been influential in the formulation of this approach. In his 1990 essay on the emerging 'underclass' in Britain, he describes them as the modern equivalent of the 'undeserving poor', and blames declines in moral standards and the 'nanny' welfare state for the lack of family cohesion, which in turn leads, in his view, to idleness and crime. The rhetoric has been echoed by politicians from the Right in Britain. Thus, John Major as Prime Minister has more than once suggested that homeless people sleep rough because they want to (BBC Radio 4 *Today* programme, prior to the general election in 1992, and again in April 1994); beggars are described as an eyesore which should be dealt with by the law (John Major again, in May 1994); and there has been a succession of similar pronouncements by government ministers about teenage mothers 'who jump the housing queue', and jobless 'shirkers' who 'live off the state' at taxpayers' expense. These provide a superficial justification for the further targeting and 'reform' of welfare. The splitting of good citizens who contribute to and reap the benefits of modern society from the undeserving underclass who threaten social stability is based on the premise that position in the social structure is individually achieved. Thus, the social class, gender, and other dimensions of structural inequality in society do not exist, and they certainly do not result in the exclusion of sections of the population from participation in the national wealth. Margaret Thatcher set the scene when she said in an interview in 1987:

'There is no such thing as society; there are only individual men and women and there are families'.

Young people tend, therefore, to be presented in political and media rhetoric according to a series of stereotypes, almost entirely negative ones (and so indeed are their families, as we shall see). This seems to occur whenever young people become visible. Stan Cohen's analysis of the Mods and Rockers phenomenon of the mid-1960s is relevant here. It is hard to imagine now the anxiety which such phenomena caused. There were fears in the 1960s of a 'Generation War', for example. Cohen explained how such 'folk devils' were created and 'moral panics', out of all proportion to the situation, could then ensue, and he foretold (Cohen 1973:204):

> More moral panics will be generated and other, as yet nameless, folk devils will be created. This is not because such developments have an inexorable inner logic, but because our society as presently structured will continue to generate problems for some of its members – like working class adolescents – and then condemn whatever solution these groups find.

The nameless folk devils of Cohen's future became the named folk devils of today. It may seem somewhat surprising that this time they are among the most vulnerable groups in society.

The current government presents homeless young people as 'choosing' to sleep rough, and therefore responsible for their own circumstances, rather than as victims of inequality and social injustice. Youth homelessness is thus constructed as an expression of youth culture and a threat to inter-generational social stability. Moral panics are applied to homeless young people such that homelessness is increasingly seen as a problem for society rather than a problem of – and created by – society. In the roofless, the visibility required in a 'folk devil' is clearly and painfully present, and the solution to rooflessness can easily become to sweep the human litter off the streets. Homelessness becomes defined in the media as a problem for those who have to witness it, rather than for those who have to experience it.

The rhetoric stressing 'traditional' values is difficult to combat. As Giddens has recently indicated (1994), in the modern world, 'tradition' defies logic, requires no defence, discourages dialogue, and is invented for the purpose of power. Cohen (1973) suggested that deviancy is defined and 'deviants' scapegoated in order to 'clarify normative contours'. Thus perhaps the burning of witches makes others feel more religious, and the castigation of the 'undeserving poor' might cheer up higher-rate taxpayers. As Cohen indicates above, society creates problems for its members and then blames them. However, recent attempts to brand as folk devils some of the weakest groups in our society – the jobless, teenage parents, lone mothers, beggars, and those dependent on welfare – have themselves failed to receive public approval.

In seeking to combat the stereotyping of homelessness as deviancy, some on the Left try to redress the balance by applying positive stereotypes of their own. Thus, organizations seeking more housing provision for young people may stress the 'ordinariness' of homeless young people in order to focus on housing issues rather than obscure an important issue with complexity. At a political level, the debate on young people's housing problems is polarized between those who seek to reduce housing demand (blaming the young) and those who seek to extend housing supply (blaming the government). Hostel staff too may emphasize the 'normality' of homeless young people, at least as far as the outside world is concerned. Liddiard and Hutson (1991b) indicate, however, that while agencies and projects working with homeless young people may present a picture of their 'normality' to the outside world, they may internally operate a gate-keeping system which recreates deviancy stereotypes, by distinguishing between deserving and undeserving cases for hostel provision. This kind of distinction is likely to occur wherever welfare systems, including hostel provision, are targeted and selective.

These approaches in their different ways over-simplify the problem and obstruct its solution. The cards are not stacked equally for young people: some are at greater risk than others and it is important to understand why. Countervailing sets of assumptions thus inform both policy-makers and those working with homeless people. The polarization of response to homelessness becomes a part of the phenomenon (and has been examined as such by Hutson and Liddiard, 1994).

Competing explanations?

Thatcher's comment that 'society' does not exist was a political example of a theme paralleled in sociological debate, as structuralist explanations of the social world were being challenged by 'post-modernist' theories which believed the structures and collectivities of modernity to be breaking down. Individuals were less constrained by the structures of inequality and were able to exercise more choice and develop their own biographies to a greater extent than before. At the same time, the collapse of the structures of modernity resulted in the loss of social class solidarities and family and community support. The result was that more people also faced risk at an individual level (Beck 1992). These 'post-modernist' ideas are themselves being challenged, and it is increasingly argued that the structures of modernity, including those of inequality, still influence the individual life course. The resulting thesis, known in sociology as 'high modernity', is that individual life courses are led along a 'reflexive biography' (Giddens 1991), in which agency (self-determination) and structure interact in a dynamic way. This is, in a sense, the middle road. Individuals are thus responsible for their own actions within the structure of opportunity which is available to them, and this varies between individuals in an unequal way (see also

Jones and Wallace 1992 for a fuller explanation of the relevance of these theories to the study of youth).

The concept of strategy becomes useful here. The notion of 'survival strategies', or ways of responding to and attempting to avoid perceived risk, helps us to understand the relation between individual action and opportunity structure which again reconciles the apparent polarities of agency and structure. Thus, social class solidarities develop as a response to the creation and reproduction of social class inequalities. More relevant to the subject of this book, though (since young people have always tended to lack possibilities for collective action), young people leaving home and facing inequalities of opportunity in the housing market adopt strategies for increasing their chances in the housing market, young people who have nowhere to live adopt strategies for survival in the open, and young people without any money may beg. These strategies tend to be at an individual rather than a collective level. Often in such situations the aim of the strategy adopted is short-term, and it is not always a matter of rational and conscious choice. 'Strategy' is thus not used here in its original sense as conscious, informed and rational choice with a longer-term positive aim, as in a game of chess or war (see Crow 1989b for a discussion). A survival strategy may not involve any of these. However, it does allow a view of the world in which people are capable of individual action and exercise a degree of choice within a structure of constraint. These ideas will be taken further in this book, and the tensions between choice and constraint, and agency and structure, will be ongoing themes.

It is one of the purposes of this book to show the roles played by social institutions and the structure of society in formulating patterns of leaving home and in structuring access to housing and employment, as a result of which all young people face increased risk in the housing market when they leave home, though only a few face homelessness. The book will examine the extent to which strategies of risk avoidance can be employed. This follows an argument expressed elsewhere (Jones and Wallace 1992) that two processes are occurring, whereby young people as a social group are increasingly marginalized, while inequalities among the young are increasing. The result is that while the risks for all young people have increased, some are excluded from participation in society.

The changing structural context

State support for the transition to adulthood has been withdrawn as the responsibility of families to provide the building blocks of citizenship is stressed and extended. The policy is based on a belief that the 'nanny state' should withdraw, and that families should be internally supportive (we see the same policy emerging in the community care concept), families being the basic social grouping. In any discussion about young people's opportunities and constraints, their families now play a crucial role. According to the Conservative Government of John Major, this function is one of social control as well as social support. Both of these are increasingly privatized onto the family. The policy is based on a lack of understanding about how parental control functions in families, and it ignores the importance of emancipation from parental control as one of the most important factors in the development of individual adult responsibility. Young people rehearse the rights and responsibilities they will hold as adult citizens first within their families, before they are enacted in the 'outside world'. Emancipation from parental control and economic independence from parents are therefore prerequisites for citizenship. Neither of these is currently supported by the state which shows increased reluctance to enter into a social contract with the younger generation of its people, and yet blames them for this omission.

Young people who are trying to leave home and live in independent households are facing particular problems in the UK in the present day. We are seeing a completely new configuration of events and trends, which may become the building bricks for new opportunities but also present young people with new problems needing new and radical solutions. Instead of responding to this challenge, however, a succession of Conservative governments has exacerbated the problem. Some commentators have identified a 'lost generation' of young people, who as time passes are becoming excluded from employment, excluded from housing, and in general terms excluded from both the rights and the responsibilities of citizenship.

So what changes have been taking place? I will concentrate on four elements all affecting young people's access to the rights and responsibilities of citizenship: access to an income from employment, access to the state safety net of social security, access to family support, and access to independent housing (see Jones and Wallace 1992 for a fuller review). These interact to affect the transition to independent living.

Access to an income from employment

Ever since state education was established, the period of time spent in education has been extended as the minimum school leaving age has increased. Greater opportunities for further and higher education have resulted in more and more people staying on in full-time education beyond the minimum school leaving age of 16 years. Whilst access to education is crucial if structural inequalities are to be redressed through social mobility, access to employment is equally important for those who cannot capitalize on extended education. Employment has become more difficult to achieve. Youth unemployment had reached such high levels by the 1980s that training schemes were extended to take young people out of the dole queues and give them training for jobs, though in practice some schemes have done little more than soak up the unemployment statistics. There are times when the right to education and training is stressed to the detriment of the right to work. Though better education is seen as a prerequisite of a classless society, other work-related routes to success are undervalued.

A wage from work has traditionally been important as the means through which economic independence has been achieved in youth, and it has been described as 'the key to citizenship' (Pateman 1989; Jones and Wallace 1992). Leaving home and other transitions to adulthood, such as the formation of partnerships and families, may all depend on a viable income from work (Willis 1984; Wallace 1987). For young people seeking a place in the labour market, access to full-time employment offering a viable independent income has become more restricted. Not only are there fewer opportunities within a shrinking youth labour market, but those that exist are likely to be worse paid and more insecure, as a result of the abolition of the Wages Councils and the withdrawal of employment protection, and the increase in part-time and casual working.

Changes in the structures of education, training and employment have re-shaped the transition from school to work into a more complex and extended pattern. The change has been particularly dramatic for the working-class school-leaver. Instead of a direct status transition from school pupil to worker, there are now more people in the intermediate statuses of trainee or student. Indeed, the expectation in the early 1980s was that all 16–18-year-olds would become students or trainees, with the erosion of the youth labour market. As we know, the youth training schemes have never worked sufficiently effectively to produce a universal status of trainee among under-18s leaving full-time education, and so other statuses, such as 'waiting for a Youth Training place', still persist (see Maclagan 1992 for example). Nevertheless, despite its failures in practice, the policy prevails.

Even if the 'training guarantee' policy (which replaced Income Support for 16–18-year-olds) had proved effective, there would still be problems. Trainee allowances are very low and do not cover housing costs, and so many working-class young people are finding that the period of their childhood dependency has been extended, and may have to fall back on financial support from their parents, postponing their transition to independent households.

Inequalities are perpetuated even among those able to benefit from the extension in education. State support for students has been eroded as parental responsibilities have been stressed. Thus, the real value of grants has decreased, while the introduction of student loans means that many students face debts soon after enrolment on their courses. Further education students tend not to leave home to study, but many of those in higher education have to leave home to go to college (though this is less common in Scotland than in England and Wales). Changes in the social security regulations during the 1980s resulted in the withdrawal of the right of students to claim Income Support during vacations, and the withdrawal of Housing Benefit. Students living away from home are particularly adversely affected. More have to take on part-time work in order to continue their courses, but more also drop out of courses. The expansion of education has therefore tended to favour those who can obtain financial subsidies from their parents.

Access to the state safety net

Parental support has become more important because the safety net of state support is being withdrawn from young people. In practice, they have never had a secure foothold in the state welfare system, precisely because they are in the process of transition from dependence to independence. Ever since the inauguration of the welfare state with the Beveridge Report fifty years ago, there has been a link between people's contribution to the welfare state and their right to benefit from it. There is thus a mechanism according to which rights are defined and legitimated. This is a legacy of the Poor Law concept of deserving as opposed to undeserving poor. Young people have always been in a very anomalous position in this respect. As their period of economic dependence is extended, their ability to contribute in a conventionally-recognized way is withdrawn. They are in a similar position to women: in both cases there is still no social and economic recognition of non-labour market contributions (Lister 1990). Young people's employment while still at school, and their contribution to the household economy while they are still formally classed as dependents, are still not recognized. Lacking employment in the formal labour market, they have no access to the rights of taxpayers. Dependence is castigated by a government which stresses the duty of citizens to stand on their own two feet, yet dependence in youth has been extended.

Since 1979 there has been a whole host of measures, the combined effect of which has been to whittle away at young people's emerging and barely-recognized rights as individuals and to make them dependent on their families of origin (see Roll 1990; Harris 1989). This is perceived by policy-makers and ideologists of the Right to be preferable to dependence on a 'nanny state'. The changes have further affected young people's prospects of citizenship (Jones and Wallace 1992).

The main changes affecting young people's transitions out of their parental homes were in 1988: the withdrawal of Income Support from under-18s (with the replacement of the 'training guarantee') and the introduction of a lower-than-adult rate of Income Support for 18–24-year-olds; the withdrawal of Unemployment Benefit from under-18s; and the abolition of the distinction between householders and non-householders in social security payments. The 1980s also saw the abolition of Exceptional Needs Payments (which met minimal furniture and equipment needs of those setting up home on social security). The 1989 introduction of Severe Hardship payments for under-18s who could prove an exceptional case, and later Social Fund loans for exceptional needs, have not satisfied the continuing demand. As a result of these changes, young people's incomes from social security have been reduced or withdrawn. Some young people are without any income (as Kirk *et al.*'s study in Edinburgh found, 1991) and support for the leaving home transition has become very difficult to obtain. Those setting up home may be able to obtain housing but find themselves living in an empty flat (see Chapter 5).

These policies have effectively extended dependency to the age of 18 and semi-dependency to the age of 25 years. They assume that anyone below that age can obtain financial support from their families. In England and Wales, young people can only leave home before the age of 18 with their parents' permission. Before then, they derive their rights, including their right to housing, from their parents. In Scotland, however, the situation is more complex. Young people have the right to leave home at 16 years without their parents' permission, and indeed need their parents' permission to stay at home, since they only live there after the age of 16 as licensees. They do, however, have the right to apply for council housing, and to sign contracts such as tenancy agreements (whereas young people in England and Wales have to have an adult rent guarantor until they are 18 years of age). In Scotland, therefore, young people are treated as 'more' adult than they are in the rest of Britain, but this creates different sets of problems. They are treated no differently from others in Britain as far as social security is concerned.

The assumption that young people living at home are dependent on their parents and subsidized by them 'explains' why trainees do not receive an allowance for their housing costs, and why housing-related benefits have been withdrawn. The abolition of the householder/non-householder distinction in the 1988 social security regulations (following earlier withdrawal of the contributions for 'board money') 'fits' within the same ideology – that non-householders are dependents, have no housing costs and are not entitled to benefits in their own right. Yet research has indicated that in fact nearly all young people in Britain who have left full-time education and are living at home do pay housing costs, in the form of board money (Jones 1991; and see also Allatt and Yeandle 1986, 1992). It is thus not only young people leaving home who have been affected by recent social security changes, but also those still living in the parental home.

Access to family support

The outcome of policies privatizing the welfare of young people onto their families by extending parental responsibilities is that family support is now a crucial factor in determining young people's life chances, and those without it are at great risk. Yet, for a variety of reasons, access to family support may have become more difficult. The effects of the recession, of high rates of unemployment and part-time working, mean that many families have little money to spare and may need their adult children to be economically independent. The increased diversity in family structure means that many young people are leaving homes in which they are living with one parent, or a step-parent, rather than with both their natural parents. The incidence of poverty among lone parents is well documented (see, for example,

Hardey and Crow 1991), and a young person living with a lone parent may well have difficulty in seeking a subsidy from them. In the case of families which have experienced re-marriage following marital breakdown, the difficulty may lie in identifying which parent would be responsible for the provision of financial support. Family breakdown clearly has implications for the provision of support to young people, but as yet we know little about what these implications are (see Chapter 5).

For the last 35 years, concern has been expressed in many industrialized countries about the 'demise of the family'. These concerns, though long-standing, have recently taken on the dimensions of a moral panic in Britain. The concerns expressed over the years have changed little: greater equality of the sexes 'threatens' the traditional nuclear family, which depended on a separation of male and female roles (Beck 1992). The demise of the nuclear family has thus been attributed over the years to the increased participation of women in the formal labour force (Goode 1982), the availability of birth control (Dennis and Erdos 1992), and the relaxation of divorce laws. With greater gender equality, there have been shifts in parental and marital roles. Some, mainly on the Right, say that these have been supported if not encouraged by state welfare policies, while others point to the increased emphasis on individual choice within a market-led economy (Beck 1992). At all events, family structures are less likely to conform to the 'normative' nuclear framework observed during the period following the Second World War, a framework within which breadwinner husbands supported their dependent wives and children (and on which the welfare state was based). According to the General Household Survey 1991, the proportion of households in Britain conforming to the nuclear family type fell from 31 per cent in 1979 to 25 per cent in 1991, while the proportion of families headed by lone parents increased from 8 per cent to 19 per cent during the same period (OPCS 1993). According to Roll (1993), there are more lone parent families in Britain than in any other European Union (EU) country.

It is simplistic to infer from changing family structures that family relationships have also changed. As Beck (1992) pointed out in a useful theatrical analogy: family structure is the stage and family relationships the play. A different stage does not necessarily indicate that the play has changed as well. Evidence that the family is in decline frequently cites the rise in rates of juvenile crime and teenage pregnancy (though teenage pregnancy rates have decreased in Britain in recent years). Absent fathers are blamed for not fulfilling their parental responsibilities (Dennis and Erdos 1992) in the face of a widespread assumption that 'committed and stable parenting' is essential for the production of 'quality children'. Halsey (1992:xii), while admitting that the traditional family was by no means perfect, argues that: 'Nevertheless, the traditional family system was a coherent strategy for the ordering of relations in such a way as to equip children for their own eventual adult responsibilities'. The investigation into the relationship between family breakdown, poverty, crime and teenage pregnancy is ongoing. An absent father may be preferable to a 'bad' father, for example. Poverty may lead both to family breakdown and to crime. While the hierarchical structure of the nuclear family provided clear lines of responsibility and dependency, the increasing variety of family and household forms requires a restructuring of welfare provision to ensure that individuals within families have access to welfare.

Instead of increasing access to welfare for family members, the family policies of the New Right attempt to make families serve the system. While asserting the need to support 'traditional family life', in practice, family relations are increasingly being policed. In an attempt to discourage family breakdown, lone parents have been criticized and the ongoing responsibilities of absent fathers stressed. Parents are blamed for juvenile crime and held responsible for their children's misdeeds (see Allen 1990 for a critique). And, as we have seen, the responsibility of parents to provide economic support to their young has been extended. But the ideology denies the crucial (and indeed traditional) role of the family in *assisting* the emancipation of its young. Some parents, given support themselves, may be able to provide more support to their young; others lack the emotional or economic equipment to do so. Policies aimed at highlighting the responsibilities of parents may result in more family breakdown – not just in the relationships between parents, but in those between parents and their children. This will become apparent in the course of the book.

Access to independent housing

In the last few decades, there have been changes in the housing market behaviour of young people, partly because more young single people were leaving home and setting up independent homes alone or with their peers prior to marriage. The increase in student numbers exacerbates the situation. As a result, there are greater and more varied demands on the housing market, but choice in the housing market is effectively decreasing as young people are having more trouble competing for the diminishing and less varied stock. Briefly, there has been a shift from public-sector rented housing into home-ownership, supported by government subsidies. This has resulted in a polarization between on the one hand home-ownership to which more and more people aspire, and on the other hand diminishing public-sector rented housing increasingly targeted towards social housing, which is becoming more and more stigmatized. There have been other trends and blips, and the recent housing recession in the South-East of England has made home-ownership less attractive and more imbued with risk than it had appeared to be before. The overall trend has resulted, however, in housing becoming less available to young people leaving home, unless they achieve a fit with the increasing polarization of the supply-side of the housing market, being rich enough to buy or poor enough to qualify for social housing.

Affordable housing and citizens' incomes

The four aspects of change described briefly above: access to an income from employment, access to the state safety net, access to family support and access to independent housing, all interact in determining the position of young people in the housing market. Those concerned with the housing needs of young people leaving home frequently draw on the notion of 'affordable housing'. The term 'affordability' is used here as a quality of the economic relationship between the supply side and the demand side of the housing market. For housing to be affordable, there must thus be an adjustment between housing costs and young people's ability and willingness to pay them (Kearns 1992). The economic competitiveness of young people in the housing market is therefore as important as supply-side factors.

The question of the social adequacy of current incomes in youth has become important, especially in the light of increased poverty among the young. It is difficult to determine the levels of income required in order to be able to make a successful transition to adult independent citizenship, but it is important to recognize that the adequacy of incomes depends on domestic circumstances and levels of domestic responsibility. In the context of women's wages, Siltanen (1986, 1994) has drawn a useful comparison between full adult ('citizens') wages which permit the costs of living in an independent household, and 'component' wages which assume access to income from other household members and do not cover the costs of independent living. The concept thus goes beyond the householder and non-householder distinction, to take into account economic roles and responsibilities within households. If we first extend the component wage concept to all income from official sources – wages, grants and benefits – and then apply a longitudinal perspective, the concept becomes useful for examining the adequacy of income levels in youth. Component incomes need to be subsidized to allow independent living, but state subsidies are being withdrawn and subsidies from families are becoming more crucial. We can develop a conceptual model (Figure 1.1) with axes reflecting two transition processes: the transition from parental home to independent housing; and the transition from component income to full adult income.

Young people tend to progress from the parental home to an independent one, and from a component income to a full one (Figure 1.1). According to a model of economic rationality, young people would move from group A to group D, in other words, not leaving the parental home until they are in receipt of a full citizen's income. However, progress to adulthood is rarely so rationally ordered, and people may find themselves in other situations. They may leave home but subsequently lose their jobs. They may have lost their homes but retain their jobs. Those in C, trying to live independently while on a component income are either living in poverty or having to find strategies for survival.

In the following chapters, I shall be considering what happens when

Figure 1.1 Citizens' incomes

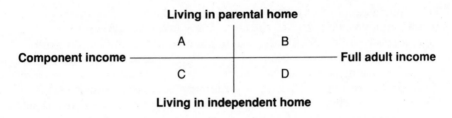

young people are trying to live independently on component incomes. Following Pickvance and Pickvance's (1994b) analysis, they may seek to improve their position in the housing market through strategies aimed at mobilizing or pooling their resources. Young people within this group would need a means of meeting the cost of independent housing on component incomes. We shall see that some may achieve this by obtaining help from their parents, by forming partnerships or by the strategy of creating households in which costs are shared. Housing demands, and housing affordability, may thus be partly structured through these strategies. The withdrawal of opportunities for full adult incomes, the removal of the social security safety net, and the narrowing of opportunities in the housing market are in combination likely to have far-reaching consequences, however. In some cases, we are talking about a group of people who have no access to financial support from their partners or parents, no wages or benefits, and may have no incomes at all. In such circumstances it is not surprising if many have no homes.

Organization of the book

This book explores empirically and theoretically some of the stereotypes surrounding leaving home and its relationship with homelessness. It considers whether leaving home has been constructed as a problem when it should be seen as a normal part of growing up, and whether this has any bearing on the emergence of homelessness as one of the major social problems of late twentieth-century Britain. I hope thus to provide policy-makers, practitioners and researchers with a greater understanding of the phenomenon of leaving home, to put homelessness in context, and to make some recommendations for the prevention of homelessness in the future as well as its management now.

The book continues in Chapter 2 with a review of historical and cross-national research on patterns of leaving home. The aim is to see to what extent patterns of leaving home are socially, legally and culturally determined. Trends and changing patterns are identified, as are continuities. National variations are discussed. The idea of 'norms' and 'traditions' in patterns of leaving home is thus questioned. It is suggested that young people's reasons for leaving home sometimes receive social legitimation and sometimes do not. Social legitimation, apparently based on assumptions about normative practices, is likely to be needed before there is a willingness on the part of government or parents to support young people's transitions out of the parental home. As a result, lack of social legitimation involves a model of 'deviancy' and increases risk, including that of homelessness. The chapter identifies young people's transition out of the parental home as becoming more complex and extended, but with echoes from Victorian times, while revealing a new pattern involving a far greater likelihood of returns to the parental home.

In the following chapters evidence is introduced from a new in-depth study of leaving home, housing and homelessness. Current patterns of leaving home in Britain are explored in Chapter 3, which reflects on whether young people's housing rights, and thus their success in the housing market, depend on social legitimation of their leaving home. It examines the construction of 'risk' in relation to the reasons young people left home and the ages at which they did so, using survey data. It considers the extent to which leaving home is a question of constraint or of choice, and questions the notion that leaving home can easily be regulated by social policies encouraging young people to delay their home-leaving, by parents, or by young people themselves.

Chapter 4 evidences and discusses the increasingly common practice of returning home, and considers the circumstances in which returning home represents a failed transition and the circumstances in which it might be desirable. It argues that families cannot always be assumed to be safe havens. The changing structures of families and increasing numbers of step-parents can – though not inevitably – make the transition from home more difficult and restrict opportunities to return. The chapter uses survey and case study material to examine the legitimacy of returns home, and whether young people have a right of abode in their parents' homes once they have left them. Strategies needed in order to effect a return home are identified and discussed. It is argued that for many, however, returning home may represent an unwelcome return to childlike dependency and is therefore to be resisted.

Similar problems relating to accessing family support are discussed in Chapter 5, which argues that access to family support, though crucial to young people leaving home, is unequal. Young people already disadvantaged by the withdrawal of state support may be doubly disadvantaged when their families are unable or unwilling to support them. Findings from national surveys are again supplemented with qualitative interview data, to reveal more about the complex negotiations involved. Because of the changing nature of the relationship between young people and their parents during adolescence and early adulthood, family support may be at its least forthcoming when it is most needed; that is, among the youngest home leavers who left because of family conflict and who cannot get access to state support. As was the case with returning home, young people may resist asking for help or accepting help which is offered at a time when they are focused on trying to prove their ability to be independent.

Chapter 6 presents a demand-side view of the 'youth housing market' through young people's experiences of housing and homelessness, and is based on survey material. It explores the relationship between family, household and housing careers. It considers young people's access to housing either in the market or in the family home. The appropriateness of new housing initiatives, such as foyers or shared flats, is discussed, as are young people's own housing strategies for improving their market positions. Housing and homelessness careers are considered, and found to be complex. How do people escape homelessness (does the system intervene to reduce inequalities or reproduce and perpetuate them, by maintaining a gate-keeping role)?

Three case study biographies are presented in Chapter 7. These begin to summarize the main themes of the book, and allow further exploration of some of the problems and issues associated with leaving home, the assumptions underlying much policy and practice, and the main issues which this book covers (choice and constraint, the responsibilities of families and the state, and the needs of young people as they become citizens). Chapter 8 presents a summary, and briefly discusses the implications for policy and practice. The appendices contain further information about the programme of research on which this book is based, and on the data sources which provide the new empirical evidence presented.

Chapter 2
Trends and 'tradition'

The previous chapter discussed the concepts which entangle the expression 'leaving home', and described some of the policy structures which have shaped recent patterns of transition out of the parental home, suggesting that these have contributed to the increased likelihood of failure to gain a foothold in the housing market. It argued that leaving home has been 'problematized', so that its social meanings have changed and become more closely linked with homelessness; and so that there is a polarization between those who believe the responsibility for homelessness lies in changing patterns of leaving home and those who see the responsibility as lying in the supply side of the housing market. The purpose here is to consider the validity of the models of deviancy and normality which have been attached to patterns of leaving home. In the following pages, historical and cross-national research will throw light on the ways practices vary between societies and social groups, and change over time, calling into question the notion of traditional and normative models of behaviour, and thus deviant models too.

Tradition and social legitimation

Citizenship involves a package of rights and responsibilities which accumulate during youth as young people progress from an indirect relationship with the state, mediated by their parents, to a direct relationship as adults (Jones and Wallace 1992). It is a concept which allows us to consider young people's transitions to adulthood in terms of the social institutions and social structures of inequality which shape the transition process into its varying forms, and to examine the extent to which there is self-determination, within these structural constraints, in youth. Claims on housing rights thus involve both of these: rights being conferred from the top down, while claims are made from the bottom up. Access to rights is a further problem, since though rights may in theory be universal, access to them may be limited (see Coles, forthcoming 1995, on the rights of young people in disadvantaged groups). Thus, young people leaving home are making claims on the basis of their understanding of their housing rights, but their claims may be not officially validated. Rights are problematic. Young people's rights even more so.

The question of rights is increasingly a global concern, as the United Nations takes up the issues of specific disadvantaged groups, such as refugees, or children (the UN Convention on the Rights of the Child). Turner (1993) suggests that while a Marxist account of human rights would associate them with a 'phoney liberalism', Weber's guiding theme was the increasing rationality of law, based on social relations of power, legitimacy and discipline. Thus rights 'are part of this class struggle whereby classes appeal to substantive law to justify their claim to resources', the working class appealing to social justice, while the middle class manipulate law in the name of 'social order' (Turner 1993:494–5).

The relevance here of this debate is that given the problematic nature of young people's housing rights, and lacking both the authority of law to justify claims to housing, and the power to manipulate the law, young people may be dependent on claims on the basis of social justice. This would indicate that housing claims cannot be legitimated legally, but must be legitimated socially. Put simply, this means that, as Burton *et al.* (1989) have argued, young people leaving home for a reason which is seen as socially legitimated may be more likely to obtain access to housing than those whose reason for leaving home lacks social legitimation. Furthermore, the legislation affecting housing supply may (following Turner 1993) be manipulated by those in power so that claims on the grounds of social justice are countered with arguments based on 'tradition', which as Giddens (1994) indicated is often constructed for power purposes. Tradition and precedent may thus be invoked on both sides as grounds for social legitimation.

We shall see in this chapter how the 'normative' pattern of leaving home is a comparatively modern construct and how current patterns of leaving home, far from being deviant, reflect long-standing practices. The chapter also considers tradition in an international context. We can begin to understand why leaving home has become more problematic. Are young people's current demands for housing legitimated by historical precedent, or are new patterns emerging? What are the implications of recent trends for young people, their families and society? The chapter first provides a historical perspective to research on leaving home in Britain, and then reviews research on more recent patterns in other countries, mainly European.

Historical research

Social historians in Britain have the advantage of access to rich data sources for which most other countries have no equivalent. Census data or documents indicating patterns of co-residence in households in Britain have allowed the analysis of household composition for several hundred years. There is a disadvantage, though, that the dynamic character of leaving home as a transition, or process, out of the parental home may be lost because of the use of cross-sectional 'snapshot' data sources.

Nevertheless, it is through the historical research that we can identify separate, though related, strands in the transition to adulthood:

- the transition from education into the labour market
- the transition from parental home to marital home
- the transition from being a child to being a parent.

Underlying all of these is the transition from dependence to citizenship. Over time, the nature of the relationship between these basic transitions has changed. The general trend from prior to the industrial revolution had been for these three strands of transition to become more and more closely related, until by the 1950s they reached their most condensed and integrated form (Jones and Wallace 1992). This was at the time when Parsons (1956) and Coleman (1961) were commenting on youth and family life in the US, and the 'functionalist' view came to prominence in the sociology of the day. The consequence has been for patterns of family life, including patterns of transition to adulthood, identified in the 1950s and 1960s to be considered as normative, but research on earlier periods show that they were a new phenomenon.

Protracted transitions

Earlier 'norms' had been quite different. Two main points emerge from the studies of patterns immediately prior to the industrial revolution in Britain and for more than a century after it: first, that the transition out of the parental home was frequently protracted; second, that it often included a stage between the parental home and the marital one. In other words, there was a process of leaving home, during which young people entered 'intermediate' households. We shall see that these two patterns, discussed below, have persisted into modern times.

In pre-industrial times, according to Laslett (1971:15), children often left the parental home at an early age (often, he estimated, around the age of 10) to live as servants in another household; they may then have spent fifteen years or more with that family before marrying and forming their own households. Eighteenth century adolescence was, according to Wall (1987), characterized by mass movement from the parental home, as young people left in search of employment as servants or into lodgings. Anderson's (1971, 1983) and Wall's (1978) research on patterns in the mid-nineteenth century show that a large proportion of young people still left home in adolescence to live in their employers' households as servants or apprentices, or to move into the towns and take up board and lodging with a family. Again, marriage was likely to occur later, when young people were in their twenties and more able to afford it.

Modell and Hareven (1973) found similar patterns in nineteenth century America, and infer, from the age differences between boarders and their landlords, that boarding was often chosen as a 'family surrogate' by men and women in their early twenties who moved into the towns. The 'lodger evil' was blamed by some contemporaries for overcrowding of homes and moral decline, and the incidence of boarding decreased in the US by the end of the century.

The historical research suggests, then, that many young people, though leaving home at an early age, were not living in newly-formed households or independent housing, but in 'intermediate households' (Jones 1987a). Leaving home was not necessarily, therefore, related to independent adult status, but reflected a level of continued economic and social dependence. Adult status and separate independent housing was more likely to be gained much later, at the time of marriage and family formation. Unlike these later transitions, leaving home was not dependent on a very high level of economic resources. Nevertheless, social class differences developed over time. Before the eighteenth century, the children of both the gentry and pre-industrial workers left home at an early age. Gradually, however, it became the practice of children of the gentry to stay longer in the parental home (Wall 1978), while the children of labourers left earlier to take up employment. Daughters tended to leave home earlier than sons, though the reasons for this gender difference are unclear (Wall 1987).

There were also spatial differences. Comparing data for the years between 1697 and 1841, Wall concluded (concurring with Anderson 1971) that the conditions of life in large towns by the mid-nineteenth century resulted in children remaining in their parental households both for longer than they had in pre-industrial England, and for longer than their contemporaries in rural areas (Wall 1978:193). It is interesting to note that the urban/rural difference prevalent in the nineteenth century can still be observed in the present day, with young people from the remote rural areas of Scotland far more likely than those in the towns to leave both their parental homes and their community, in search of work or to study (Jones 1992a).

'Normative' condensed transitions

In the period following the Second World War, new patterns of leaving home developed, and, as argued above, these have come to be regarded as normative. Wall (1978) contrasted the gradual nature of the process of leaving home in the past with the close link between leaving home and marriage in the postwar years. This was a result in part of the disappearance of the intermediate status of servant or boarder. Anderson (1983), too, has suggested that in contrast to the protracted nineteenth-century transition from childhood status to household headship, the average age gap between leaving home and becoming head of household had reduced to one year by the 1970s. Transitions during the 1950s and 1960s (the height of the functionalist era in sociology) certainly appear to have been at their most condensed, most coherent, and most unitary. Many young adults, especially those from working-class families, typically left home, married and started families within a short space of time.

By the 1960s, the age at leaving home was closely associated with the age at marriage, partly because the median age at first marriage had become lower. Indeed marriage was the most socially acceptable (legitimated) reason for leaving home. Young (1984:53) commented that: 'Marriage has maintained a long-standing dominance as the principal, traditional and acceptable reason for leaving'.

Such was the strength of the link between leaving home and marriage, that in survey analysis the age at marriage was often used as a proxy variable for the age of leaving home, as Kiernan (1985) points out. (The reliability of these survey findings, therefore, depends on whether such assumptions could be validly made.) The period in life when one was in an intermediate household situation between being the child of the household and the head (or spouse of head of household) had apparently shrunk. By the middle of the twentieth century, people no longer entered living-in apprenticeships or servant positions, and were less likely (in comparison with the nineteenth century) to be boarding or in some other intermediate or long-term housing situation between the parental home and the marital one. The 1960s, when there was probably the closest coincidence between marriage and leaving home (Kiernan 1985), was a period of relative affluence, with virtually full employment and a readily available supply of cheap rented housing suitable for young couples. It was also a time when young people had become noticed as a consumer group (Abrams 1961), when youth cultures were flourishing, and when young people were in a variety of ways making their opinions known. These latter trends were to affect patterns of family and household formation and thus change the nature of leaving home once more.

Extended transitions

There have been major changes in the transitions to adulthood in the last few decades (Jones and Wallace 1992). The overall pattern is that transitions have become more extended and complex and the link between the different transition strands has weakened. In some respects, it can be said that the overall shape of transition has returned to an earlier form (Gillis 1985). The forms of individual strands of transition have become more complex and diffuse.

Marriage patterns have changed considerably over the last twenty years, with the age at marriage first getting lower (as described above), but then rising in the 1970s, as it was increasingly preceded by cohabitation (Kiernan 1983, 1985), and as participation in further and higher education increased, and for other reasons, such as the availability of birth control and the development of more equal opportunities for (and greater expectations of) women, as a result of the women's movement. The close link between the age at marriage and that of leaving home was breaking. Cohabitation increasingly became an intermediate stage, still usually followed by marriage, and it has become more appropriate to examine the relationship between leaving home and forming *partnerships*. The terminology used henceforth in this book will reflect this change, and I shall refer to 'partnership homes' rather than marital ones.

The knock-on effect of these changes in marriage patterns and the extension of education on patterns of leaving home was immense. Increasingly, young single people left home in order to study or to work. Leaving home, partnership formation and childbirth became more spaced. The transitions of women who continued in education were delayed. In consequence, many more women and working-class men were able to experience a period of independence between the parental home and the partnership home, as the previously male and middle-class pattern of prolonged transition increasingly extended to them (Jones 1987a). In part this was a result of young people's increased desire at all levels of society to assert their identities and be independent, and in part it was because social policies caused a restructuring of the transition to adulthood.

By the 1980s, the trend (according to Harris 1983; Young 1984) was that young people were increasingly leaving their parental homes and moving into *independent* living situations prior to marriage or cohabitation with a partner. This produced a new phenomenon: the formation of single-person or peer households in youth, rather than partnership homes or intermediate households. The trend put a new set of pressures on the housing market, which mainly catered for family homes. Perhaps even more important, it meant that adulthood was being re-defined. Leaving home was gaining a new significance, independent of its relationship with family formation, and this in turn would affect the patterns of leaving home of future cohorts of young people. Harris (1983:221) suggests that:

> The young adult would no longer depend for the attainment of adult status (fully independent of his parents) upon founding his/her own nuclear family. Rather, the foundation of a family is made possible by the prior emancipation of the young adult from parental control and the creation of a period early in adult life when the individual defines him/herself independently of their familial status.

The most thorough examination of contemporary patterns of leaving home was by Christabel Young, in Australia (1974, 1984). It is from these studies that most of the more recent work has derived. Young found that the reason for leaving home was closely related to the age at leaving, with people leaving home later for marriage, and earlier for employment or educational reasons. In stark contrast to earlier studies, she found that only 31 per cent of men and 45 per cent of women *first* left home in order to marry. This gender difference was reflected in the ages at leaving: in general, young women left home two years younger than men (Young 1974), though her more recent survey showed that the age gap was diminishing. The median age at leaving home was 19.5 among women and 20.7 among men (Young 1984).

The process of leaving home

It was Young who crucially discovered that the first leaving home event was still frequently part of a *process* in the transition to independent living (though the process had changed in form and now involves returns to the parental home). Young found that those leaving home for non-marriage reasons were not only younger, but also more likely to return home again. In all, around half the men, and 40 per cent of the women who had left their parental homes later returned (Young 1984). When these returners later left home again, it tended to be in order to marry. The idea that people could leave home more than once was new. Studies which do not discriminate between the first and the most recent leaving home event may therefore over-stress the link between leaving home and marriage. This would include studies of leaving home based solely on current household data. The research has been important in indicating patterns which differed from those considered normative in the 1960s, and in particular the existence of a variety of reasons for leaving home, not all associated with household formation.

This Australian research suggests that, as in the nineteenth century, leaving home may not constitute a true move to independence and emancipation from parental authority, particularly when leaving home was not for the purpose of marriage and the formation of a new family. The relationship between leaving home and adult independence is thus brought into question (see also Jones and Wallace 1992, on the problematic nature of the concepts of dependence in the family home and independence away from it). Diana Leonard (1980), in a study of newly-weds in South Wales, questioned whether independence is really sought by the adolescent or young adult or really 'desired' by child or parents. She drew a useful distinction between 'leaving home' and 'living away from home', the latter being reversible, while the former constitutes a one-way definite breach. Like Young, she found that many absences from the parental home were short-term, and returns home were common, particularly among those who first left home in order to study or get a job, and who had been perceived as 'living away' from home in the interim.

National Child Development Study

In order to study the process of leaving home in the ways advocated by Young, longitudinal data – or at least data offering the scope for a longitudinal perspective – are needed. Such data became available with the 1981 sweep of the National Child Development Study (NCDS), a birth cohort of young people born in one week in March 1958 (Shepherd 1985). The 1981 sweep was a survey of 12,500 of the cohort at the age of 23 years, and included questions about leaving home and their subsequent housing histories. The sample size allowed class and gender analysis, and the study of inequalities in the transitions to adulthood (Jones 1987b, 1988; Kiernan 1992). From the NCDS we know, for example, that the median age at leaving home in Britain was 20 years for women and 21.9 years for men (Jones 1987a), but there were also class differences, such that the first to leave home were middle-class women and the last to leave were working-class men.

The NCDS research (Jones 1987a) showed the diversity of patterns of leaving home in Britain in the 1970s. It became clear that people left home for reasons other than marriage, and that these reasons included an increased desire for single independent living, thus confirming Harris's (1983) view and the Australian findings (Young 1984). Perhaps the most important aspect of this earlier study was the finding that as a result of social class differences in education participation, it is the middle class who leave home earliest, not the working class, but there is an important difference in class patterns. The middle class 'live away' at a younger age, while the working class leave home later and more permanently (to use Leonard's 1980 classification). This difference appears to occur because middle-class young people are more likely to 'live away' from home as students, while among the working class leaving home is more associated with marriage. Does 'living away' constitute independent living? It is likely that in Britain, as in Australia, later leaving home events are more likely to be associated with marriage and more likely to constitute definite breaks from the parental home.

Among NCDS respondents, perhaps because they were interviewed at only a little over the median age at leaving home, only 39 per cent of men and 52 per cent of women first left home in order to live as married. This tends to confirm the continued weakening of the link with marriage by the end of the 1970s. But, as Young had indicated, reasons for leaving home varied with age. The youngest male home-leavers (at 16 and 17 years of age) mainly did so in order to take up a job, while those leaving at 18–19 years were mainly students going on courses. It was the later leavers, and especially the working-class men, who mainly left home in order to marry or cohabit. Among women, the predominant reason at all ages was marriage, though the second most common reasons were the same as those of men at all ages. Women left home on average about two years before men, mainly because of the age difference in marriage observed by Young (1974).

Younger leavers also indicated that they had left home because of problems, such as overcrowding or family conflict.

Reasons for leaving home affected the types of household and housing moved into. With a greater gap between the median ages at leaving home and at marriage among the middle class (Dunnell 1979; Haskey 1983), some form of *intermediate* household stage between being the child in a household and forming a marital household had become common particularly among the middle class and/or students. Young people from working-class homes, leaving home later and forming partnerships younger, were generally still more likely to move directly into partnership homes (Jones 1987a).

Leaving home may thus be a first step in a career leading to household formation (or indeed homelessness), but it is not necessarily immediately associated with it. There may have been an increase in single-person households, but many young people live in intermediate household situations on leaving home. These include surrogate households in accommodation associated with a job or course, but they also include moving into existing households with friends or with kin. One of the most striking class differences found in the study (Jones 1987a) was in the proportions living 'with kin' and those living with friends, among those who left home for reasons other than marriage. The survey indicated that 22 per cent of working-class women and 16 per cent of working-class men moved in with relatives (compared with 9 per cent of women and 6 per cent of men in the middle class). The pattern recalls the nineteenth-century patterns of working-class migration to areas where there was employment, and the need to board with kin for both accommodation and local job information. In contrast, the middle class more frequently live with friends in shared housing (66 per cent of men and 75 per cent of women in the middle class, compared with 51 per cent of women and 47 per cent of men in the working class). Both of these situations indicate intermediate household statuses between the parental home and independent housing.

Transitional housing has always been – for better or worse – a feature of young people's household careers. Traditionally, young people who lacked economic competitiveness – such as the apprentices and servants who made the move into towns during the industrial revolution, and others on component wages since – have sought transitional housing, often in 'intermediate households' before moving into homes of their own. This phenomenon still exists. However, the demand for single or peer independent housing, and the lack of appropriate housing supply, means that young people are sometimes living in intermediate household situations not because of convenience or because they offer a supportive environment, as may have been the case in the past, but because of the lack of anything else. The problem of 'hidden homelessness' has recently been identified. Young people who cannot obtain housing are not only homeless on the streets, they may be homeless in people's houses, but still in urgent need of stability and security.

Cross-national comparisons

Over the last decade, research on leaving home has increased. Studies in other countries, particularly those in Europe, help to throw light on changing patterns in Britain. In the following pages, international trends are summarized from recent research, including research by the author using data from the Scottish Young People's Survey (SYPS) (Jones 1990). Outside Britain, as within, the timing of most young people's departure from the family home is often only partially a matter of individual choice. The structures of opportunity continue to allow choice for some and impose constraints for others.

Across Europe, there is considerable variation in patterns of leaving home. Young people leave home earliest in Denmark: by the age of 18/19, less than half of Danish women were living with their parents, compared with over two-thirds in the UK and Germany, and more in the Netherlands, France and Ireland (Kiernan 1986). Penhale's (1990) study, based on the Census, suggests that patterns in France are similar to those in England and Wales. According to Burton *et al.*'s synthesis (1989), Greece and the Netherlands show an interesting contrast: while a high proportion of young Greeks stay in the parental home until their late twenties, when they leave in order to marry, and new household formation among young single people is limited to an affluent minority, around 75 per cent of young people aged 18–25 in the Netherlands live away from their parents, and independent living is less associated with marriage.

Cross-national variation is summarized in Table 2.1, and is interesting mainly because it can tell us something about the social construction of 'norms' and legitimated practices. In most countries, the most 'traditional' and legitimated way of leaving home is to marry, and thus to move direct from the parental home to the partnership one. The legitimacy of leaving home in order to study or start a job elsewhere is becoming more recognized in many countries, for young men at least (according to Bloss *et al.* 1990, who refer to these as the 'scholastic' and 'professional' routes). The extent to which many countries provide housing for young people appears to relate closely to the level of social approval given to reasons for leaving home, and this seems to depend on the positioning of the boundary of responsibility between the family and the state within each country. Countries with a strong family ideology tend to give greatest support to leaving home in order to marry, while those with a strong welfare state are more likely to support leaving home as a single person in order to study or work. Thus, the criteria for social legitimation of leaving home vary cross-nationally, according to prevailing ideologies.

Leaving home is an integral part of the transition to adulthood. Factors affecting the transitions to economic independence and family formation, therefore, affect patterns of leaving home. Across Europe, as in Britain, there has been a decreasing link between leaving home and partnership formation, though the relationship between leaving home and marrying

Table 2.1 Changing patterns: cross-national variation

	North Europe	South Europe
Reason for leaving		
Marriage link	Weaker than in S. Europe	Stronger/decreasing
	Strongest in UK	Strong in Greece
	Weakest in Denmark	
Students living away	More than in S. Europe	Fewer
Workers Living away	More than in S. Europe	Fewer
Returning home		
Frequency	More and increasing	Less common (??)
Types	Students (vacations)	than in N. Europe
	Unemployed?	
Type of household		
Single person	More and increasing	Uncommon
Age and gender		
Age at leaving	Lower (esp. Denmark)	Higher (esp. Italy)
Gender	Women leave earlier	Women leave earlier
Source of housing		
Parental housing	Esp. working-class males	Most single people
Private housing	Young professionals	Young couples
	Students	
State housing	Young mothers	

Note: There is an additional element when we think of patterns in the ex-Soviet Union. Here there was state provision, no private market and arguably a disrupted family tradition. Young adults often stayed in the parental home until they were middle aged, married and with children of their own.
Sources: Kiernan 1986; Burton *et al.* 1989; CEC 1989, 1991; Chisholm and Bergeret 1991

remains strong in the countries of southern Europe. When marriage decreases in significance, there is an increase in the incidence of single-person households (Schwarz 1983; Jones 1990), indicating that people leave home for other reasons. Kiernan (1986) points out that this trend may depend on the availability of housing stock: thus, where housing is available, young single people may leave home earlier. The situation in Denmark, where young people leave home earliest, appears to support this hypothesis: the link between leaving home and marriage is weak, the housing needs of young single people are recognized and housing stock is more available (Haywood 1984). However, in the UK, where there is a shortage of housing, the link between leaving home and partnership formation, though still strong, is weakening (Kiernan 1986), and despite the shortage of appropriate housing, the incidence of single and peer households has increased (Jones 1987a, 1990).

Structure and constraint

Recent decades have been characterized in many countries by an extension of the period of dependency in youth, caused by an extension of education and training, shrinkage of the youth labour market, and a reduction in state support. In the UK, leaving home to go on a course is the most common reason overall for leaving home by the age of 19 years (Jones 1987a, 1990). It is likely that the expansion of opportunities for higher education is speeding up the process of leaving home as the student population increases (Kiernan 1986), and causing an indirect effect, as other groups of young people aspire to independent living and emancipation from parental control before marriage. The extent to which students live away from home varies cross-nationally, though: students in England and Wales are more likely to live away from home than students in Scotland or Germany (Jones and Wallace 1992). It also varies according to the type of course: few further education students live away from home in Britain. Leaving home to go on a course depends on having the financial resources to do so, and students are increasingly experiencing financial hardship in Britain, as the previous chapter indicated. It is becoming more difficult for students to live away from home and they may be more likely to return home in the vacations, and more likely to seek courses within travelling distance of their parents' homes.

Employment is no longer an option for many people leaving school under the age of 18 years in Britain. During the late 1970s and early 1980s, unemployment among young people grew to such levels that training schemes were extended. The 1988 social security regulations made schemes virtually compulsory for those not in employment or education. However, training allowances contain no living costs element. Leaving home in order to take up a job was, as noted, the main reason men under 18 years of age in Britain left home, both according to the NCDS (Jones 1987a), and more recently according to the Scottish Young People's Survey 1985/6/7 (Jones 1990). If employment once provided 16- and 17-year-olds with the main reason for leaving home, and fewer young people are now able to get full-time jobs, do under-18s now delay leaving home, or do they leave home anyway for other reasons?

During the 1980s, there was concern about the effects of unemployment on the transitions to adulthood and in particular household and family formation. This was reflected in the work of Claire Wallace (1987). Her study of young people on the Isle of Sheppey showed that access to employment affected patterns of transition: young people who had been unemployed were more likely to be living as dependents in the parental home than those who had been regularly employed. Failure to achieve one transition may, therefore, affect other strands of the transition to adulthood (see also Hutson and Jenkins 1987). Willis (1984) went further and argued that without a wage, young people's transition to adulthood would be impeded.

Self-determination and choice

The above are structural explanations for variation in patterns of leaving home over time, between nations and within nations. The framework within which young people make their transition to participation in society is subject to continual change, and over time new problems are posed and new constraints develop. However, there is a countervailing trend as young people are increasingly seeking to assert their independence and identity. This is where 'agency' or self-determination most obviously interacts with the structures of determinism. This 'individualism' has been reflected in changing patterns of leaving home in many countries. In Australia, independence had become the most important single reason given for leaving home among those aged under 18 years, by the 1980s (Maas 1986). The tendency to leave home in order to live independently has since been noted in West Germany (Mayer and Schwarz 1989), France (Bloss *et al.* 1990), Britain (Jones 1990), and the Netherlands (De Jong Gierveld *et al.* 1991). As the latter (1991:68) point out 'this does not mean that the other young adults do not value freedom and independence, but that they have other more or less pressing reasons for leaving home'.

Young (1984:54) suggests that this trend creates a new stage in the transition to young adulthood. Galland (1990) describes this period of 'post-adolescence' as a new age in life, a period of freedom and individualism, giving young people the opportunity to build up their social identity and construct a 'social destiny'. According to Bloss and colleagues (1990) and Beck (1992), young people have increased choice. Jones and Wallace (1990, 1992) are among those who have argued, however, that choice is not available to all, and opportunity structures are still stratified. There are few indications that even among the most advantaged groups in Britain, opportunities for informed choice have widened: rather, the market has taken over as one of the mechanisms which structure inequality, making access to resources more necessary. In the current economic crisis and housing slump, many of the young people who are managing to live in their own households face serious financial problems and have limited scope for self-expression. The ways in which they themselves speak of 'risk-taking' (see Chapters 3 and 4) indicates that it is often a dangerously uninformed and doomed strategy. This is particularly the case for those under 18 years of age who may be on low incomes from student grants, wages or training allowances, and have no entitlement to social security in Britain. 'Choice' depends on the extent to which they can mobilize personal or family resources, and 'advantage', in this context, means access to family emotional and economic support (Pickvance and Pickvance 1994b, and see Chapter 5). This may not be forthcoming.

Throughout, we see disparity between the wealthy and the poor. There are also gender differences: women leave home earlier than men in all these countries. This may be largely because of the sex difference in age at marriage or cohabitation (Baanders *et al.* 1989, commenting on the

Netherlands; Steger, 1979, commenting on West Germany), and indeed in the UK marriage or cohabitation is still the main reason overall why women leave home (Jones 1987a). It may be because they are more able to obtain public sector housing: Burton *et al.* (1989:20) point out that the increasing emphasis on social housing in Britain means that 'stated simply, pregnancy is often the quickest route to being allocated a dwelling in the social rented sector' (though as Greve, 1991, reminds us, suggestions by some British politicians on the New Right that young women become pregnant in order to obtain housing are not backed up with any evidence). It may be because daughters need to escape from home to achieve independence because of more restrictive parental authority, though some may argue that in practice the transition for many is still from economically dependent child to economically dependent wife. It may be because daughters have to take on more household tasks than sons (Jablonka *et al.* 1987, quoted in Burton *et al.* 1989), but this may also make them more capable of independent living. As gender inequalities very slowly decrease, women should become less likely to leave home in order to marry, though this does not necessarily mean that they would leave home later, and the emphasis on families with children in social housing is more likely to perpetuate gender inequality than reduce it.

Legitimacy and support

The transition out of the parental home is, according to Burton and colleagues (1989:86) likely to be easiest when the reason for leaving is seen as legitimate:

> We would like to stress that most young people manage the transition from dependent to independent living without experiencing any serious difficulties. This is especially the case when the circumstances of their leaving are seen as respectable or legitimate, for instance, when leaving home to get married, to take up a job or further education or to carry out (often compulsory) military service. Under these circumstances resources are very often available from a range of support networks, including the family, local communities and the state. Young people who make the transition under less respectable or legitimate circumstances often receive less support . . . Young people in this position are frequently held to be personally responsible for the problems they face and responses are devised, inappropriately, on this basis.

The legitimacy of leaving home for independence, or because of problems at home, is not widely established. Leonard (1980:49) suggested that in the 1970s, 'a home' is seen essentially as something which is developed by a married couple and their children . . . To 'make a home' alone or with peers is a contradiction in folk terms and difficult in practice.

In other words, it was not socially legitimated, and was contrary to normative concepts of 'home', as discussed in the previous chapter. At the time of Leonard's study, most young people who 'lived away from home' did so in hostels or with relatives, rather than in bedsits or flats shared with peers. More recently, it has become common for people to live in single households and the concept of 'home' may have become even more problematic as a result. There are few single-person households in southern Europe, where the family is seen as the main provider of housing to single people. Even in northern Europe, where such households do exist, most housing initiatives are on the fringes of the housing sector (hostels, self-build, etc.) (Burton *et al.* 1989).

However much young people may want to live independent lives, their freedom of action is limited by the structures of the family, the state, and increasingly the market, which interact, in theory at least, regulating housing demand and housing provision. One of the main sources of cross-national variation lies in the boundary of responsibility between the family and the state, as suggested earlier. According to Burton *et al.* (1989), the position of this boundary affects the extent to which the family acts as a buffer between the state and the young person, providing an alternative source of housing. In the countries of southern Europe, where families retain their 'traditional' functions, they, rather than the state or the market, are still seen as the main providers of housing to young people. Nor is the trend necessarily towards more state provision in these countries: in Spain, the period of economic dependency has been extended to 26 years and the family's burden of support thus increased; in consequence, it is more difficult for young people to set up independent households, and there is overcrowding in family homes, especially in areas of social housing.

In northern countries with a long history of welfare intervention, 'family values and family care are being re-asserted as the alternative to insensitive and profligate state agencies' (Burton *et al.* 1989:9). This is particularly the case in Britain, where 'traditional family values' have been upheld under successive Conservative governments, anxious to reduce the state's responsibility to provide alternative security (Jones and Wallace 1992). Burton and colleagues (1989:9) reported that it is nevertheless not usual to suggest that young people should stay at home longer, since it is recognized that 'frustrated departure from the family home breeds destructive and deviant attitudes which tend to hinder development to adulthood and full citizenship'. Since this was written, however, government ministers in Britain have increasingly suggested that young people should not leave home 'prematurely'. Current social security regulations (see Roll 1990) are one of the means by which young people are 'encouraged' to stay longer in the parental home, but young people may also be forced out of the family home as a result.

A postponed transition?

The continued extension of the period of dependent youth has made leaving home more difficult. Where people have a choice (i.e. there are local jobs and courses, they get on with their parents, there is room for them, etc.), they may decide to delay leaving home even if they could afford to leave. Others leave home even though they cannot afford to do so, as we shall see in the next chapter, because living at home is not an option. Leaving home may thus depend on a range of factors, from family relationships to economic circumstances and the availability of housing.

In many countries, researchers have observed changes in the age at leaving home over the last decades. De Jong Gierveld and colleagues (1991) suggest that in the Netherlands, the age at leaving home rose in the period after the war, then decreased again during the 1960s and 1970s with the increase in economic prosperity and changes in norms and values. Since 1980, however, there has been a slight increase in the age at which men left the parental home in the Netherlands (De Jong Gierveld *et al.* 1991), and this has also been found in Germany (Mayer and Schwarz 1989), France (Godard and Bloss 1988) and the US (Heer, Hodge and Felson 1984/5) (see also the findings from the *Young Europeans* studies, reported in Chisholm and Bergeret 1991, and CEC, 1982, 1989, 1991).

Again, explanations tend to be structural and determinist. One explanation of the apparent recent rise in the age at leaving home relates to the changing nature of parent–child relationships as a result of smaller family size and more space in the family home. Thus, young people have more opportunity for personal freedom and space without having to leave home (De Jong Gierveld *et al.* 1991). This explanation does not take into account the larger families and more complex relationships which may result from re-marriage and step-families (Wicks 1991) and which may be associated with leaving home earlier (Kiernan 1992, and see Chapter 3). The young people to whom the explanation may apply are likely to be those with wealthier families.

The widespread economic recession, with the loss of jobs, stagnating incomes and withdrawal of social security benefits, means that most young people no longer have the financial resources needed for independent living (Keilman 1987). A recent American study found that the proportion of young people living with their parents had increased since 1970 as a result of increasing housing costs and high rates of unemployment (van Vliet 1988, quoted in Pickvance and Pickvance 1994a). A French study (Leridon and Villeneuve-Gokalp 1988), and a British one (Wallace 1987) both found that the unemployed were more likely to be living with their parents than their employed contemporaries.

It is also argued that patterns of leaving home reflect the state of the housing market, and that the current apparent rise in the age at leaving home is a response to a lack of housing opportunity and dwindling housing stocks (Kiernan 1986). This is not only the situation in Britain. Burton *et al.* (1989), in their synthesis of the work of nine research groups across Europe, discuss the effects of gentrification on the youth housing sectors in France, where furnished digs are gradually disappearing (Bauer and Cuzon 1987), and similarly the displacement of low income households in Germany (Jablonka *et al.* 1987) and the Netherlands (Deelstra and Schokkenbroek 1988). Young people are increasingly being excluded from the housing market and forced to stay at home, or if they have already left, face the alternatives of returning home or becoming homeless. As Burton and colleagues indicate, the closure of the housing market to the majority of young people postpones the problem for some, and exacerbates the problem (of homelessness) for others. They point out (1988:38) that a growing dislocation between housing and labour market processes has occurred: there is a need for greater geographical flexibility in the labour force as Europe becomes more integrated, but housing systems are becoming more rigid (see also McLennan 1994). At an individual level, this can mean that it becomes more difficult for a young person to reconcile his or her employment and housing needs.

Returning home as part of the process

Are we really sure that the age at leaving home is increasing, though? The process of leaving home has become more complex of late (Goldscheider and LeBourdais 1986). Much of the research cited above has been based on data on current households, rather than asking people when they first left home. As originally indicated by Young (1984), people may leave home more than once, mainly because their course or job has come to an end, and/or for financial reasons. Bloss *et al.* (1990) describe the scholastic and professional routes to social autonomy as more tentative than the matrimonial route and more associated with returns to the parental home (thus representing a more experimental transition to adult life).

It is important to remember that for many young people leaving home is a process rather than a one-off event, and that it may represent a period in which there are status shifts from dependence to independence and back again. We need to consider whether these shifts represent failure of the transition out of the parental home, or whether tentative steps, testing the water, are an essential part of the process (see Chapter 4). Analysis of the NCDS indicated that of young people aged 23 living at home with their parents, one-third had previously left home at some stage to live away (Jones 1987a). This shows the extent to which use of a household structure variable to estimate age at leaving home can distort the picture. De Jong Gierveld *et al.* (1991) comment that more research is needed on the factors affecting returning home: 'the returning young adult syndrome' (or 'incompletely-launched young adults' according to Schnaiberg and Goldenberg 1989). Some research has already been done, notably by Christabel Young. Following her research in Australia, Young warns that when thinking about patterns of leaving home, we should be clear whether to invest significance in the first or last leaving home event.

Trends in leaving and returning

If changing patterns of leaving home and returning home affect levels and types of demand on the housing market, then it is important to understand the trends, but leaving the parental home is a difficult issue to measure (especially since cross-sectional surveys are not sensitive to the processes involved and tend to distort the picture). First, Young (1984) has indicated that young people's definitions may vary from those of their parents, the former being more likely to say that they have left home. Second, how do you define leaving home when young people are not first living with their parents? In a situation where a young person leaves their parental home at 14 years to go into care, and leaves care at 16, which of these events do we define as the leaving home event? And, third, in a situation where young people often leave their parental homes more than once, how do we determine whether the more important event is the first or most recent (as Young asks)? The study of leaving home is not an exact science.

Having said that, can we identify any trends in the patterns of leaving home? Data on patterns between 1985 and 1991 are contained in the SYPS series of longitudinal surveys, based on school year cohorts (see Appendix 2). These national Scottish data sets are currently the only large surveys providing information of patterns of leaving home in Britain. Figure 2.1 shows that increasing numbers of young people in Scotland are leaving home by the age of 19 years. This indicates that they are in fact leaving home earlier. However, the chart also shows that increasing numbers are returning home, and thus, one must suppose, leaving again later. These patterns have also been noted in Australia (Young, 1987). It is more likely, then, that young people are first leaving home earlier than they did in the mid-1980s, but that they may well last leave home later. Which of these events is the more significant? Well, in terms of housing, the first one is. Young people make their first demands for housing when they first leave home; though they may return, their housing needs should be recognized from the time of the first, rather than the last, leaving home event. Increased homelessness suggests that in practice they are not recognized.

The pattern of leaving home earlier has implications for parents as well. It means, in demographic terms, that parents enter the post-parental phase of their life course earlier, though, with the increase in marital breakdown, young people are more likely to leave a home in which they live with a lone parent or a step-parent. Kiernan (1985) comments on the 'demographic

Figure 2.1 Changing pattern of leaving home, 1987–91, SYPS

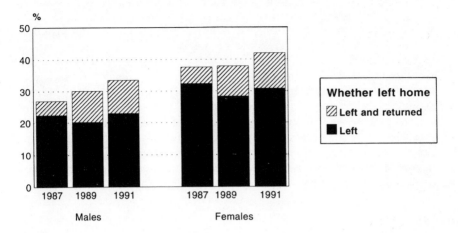

Source: SYPS 1985/87, 1987/89, 1989/91

irony' that young people are leaving home earlier at a time when there is an increased possibility that middle-aged couples will be taking on responsibility for aged parents. Thus earlier departure of children from the parental home may prevent the necessity for parents to have simultaneous responsibility for their children and their own parents in their middle years. Leaving home, therefore, reduces the potential stress on parents.

In this chapter, we have seen that leaving home is a process and has usually been a protracted one, increasingly involving returns home. Whereas in the 1950s and 1960s, leaving home was almost always associated with marriage, young people now also leave home for other reasons, such as to study, to work or because they want to live independently like their peers. The transition out of the parental home has changed from being one-way to being reversible, as young people increasingly return home as part of the process, and therefore leave home more than once. The establishment of an independent home, the ultimate outcome of leaving home, on the other hand continues to involve a complex configuration of intermediate housing and household statuses.

In the following chapters, patterns of leaving the parental home are considered in relation to patterns of returning home. Now more than ever it seems that people (and especially younger ones) are returning home because of economic or housing problems after leaving it, and that the age at first leaving home has reduced, as more people set out in search of independence, even if they are less likely to achieve it. Though, as argued earlier, governments may seek to regulate and delay entry into the housing market through education, training, employment, social security and housing policies, they are not necessarily successful. Young people still attempt to leave home and may set up independent households in their teenage years, despite official discouragement to do so. Explanations of patterns of leaving home, therefore, need to take account of the role of the individual within the context of structurally-determined risk, choice and opportunity.

This chapter has considered the notion of social legitimation, which contains both the concept of 'the right way' to leave home, which is more likely to attract societal and family support, and the concept of 'deviancy' which in contrast produces a moral panic and withdrawal of support. It has indicated how ideas about norms and deviancy are socially, nationally and temporarily specific, and how patterns of leaving home, along with other aspects of the process of transition to adulthood, respond to and are affected by changing structures of risk and opportunity. The next chapter explores how, nevertheless, ideas about tradition and normative practices affect risk, and are internalized by young people themselves.

Chapter 3
Leaving home

The first step in the process of household formation is leaving the parental home, and so it is to current patterns of leaving home that we now turn. The last chapter indicated that concepts of 'normative' and 'deviant' behaviour are socially constructed but are slow to respond to changing practice. The hypothesis proposed was that reasons for leaving home which have not been socially legitimated are less likely to receive support and therefore more associated with risk in the housing market than the traditional and legitimated reasons for leaving home. This issue is explored further in the following pages. The chapter considers whether the timing of leaving home, and thus housing demand, can be regulated by young people and their families, and whether concepts of 'premature' or 'delayed' departure from the parental home bear any relation to practice. We shall see how, though moral ideas about patterns of leaving home are internalized by young people themselves, they do not necessarily affect their actions.

The findings presented here and in the following chapters mainly come from the Scottish Young People's Surveys (SYPS), follow-up interviews at 21 years with a subset of the cohort selected as case studies on criteria of 'risk' in the housing market, and a 1992 survey of homeless young Scots aged 16–22 years (see Appendix 2). Where possible I have compared the SYPS findings with earlier ones from the National Child Development Study (NCDS) 1981, in order to provide some indication of whether Scottish findings can be generalized to the British case. It is worth stressing though that there are currently no comparable data on England and Wales, and so the SYPS, which was discontinued in 1993, is all we have to go by.

The age at leaving home

Age is a factor affecting access to many aspects of citizenship: education grants, training allowances, social security, and wage levels are all age-structured. As a result many young people live on component incomes which do not sustain independent living, as discussed in Chapter 1. The younger people are when they leave home, the more risk they are likely to face because, whatever their other circumstances, they are prevented by their age from gaining access to full independent adult incomes. Age, there-fore, is a dimension of inequality and important in the construction of risk. Young people leaving home under the age of 18 are thus most adversely affected by age-grading of income opportunities.

Lack of good national British data makes it impossible to give an accurate figure for the current median age at leaving home. The NCDS 1981 showed that the median age for the 1958 birth cohort was 20 years for women and 21.9 years for men. The SYPS 1987/89 indicates that over one-third of young people in Scotland have left home by the age of 19 and around one in ten by the time they are 18 years of age. (Figure 3.2, p. 50 will indicate the drift away from the parental home with age.) There are, as Chapter 2 indicated, social class and gender differences in the timing of leaving home, with working-class men generally leaving home last. This is reflected in young people's expectations as well as their actions: among 19-year-old Scots living with their parents, working-class men were the least likely to be planning to leave (Jones 1990). Within these overall patterns of leaving home, it is not, however, uncommon for young people to leave home in their teenage years, even though the current climate is generally less favourable to their doing so.

Reasons for leaving home

We saw in the previous chapter how the link between leaving home and marriage is being weakened as young people increasingly leave home in order to take up a job or to study. The legitimacy of these reasons – particularly the latter – is becoming established. In recent years it has become apparent that people are leaving home for other reasons which still seem to lack social legitimation: independence and in order to get away from problems at home.

Figure 3.1 shows the reasons young Scots left home, according to their age and sex. The chart shows how reasons for leaving change as young people become older, so that younger people leaving home are more likely to do so because of family problems, or to start a job, while 17- and 18-year-olds are more likely to be leaving home to go on a course. By the age of 19 years, relatively few have left home in order to live with a partner.

Figure 3.1 Reasons for first leaving home by age first left and sex, SY

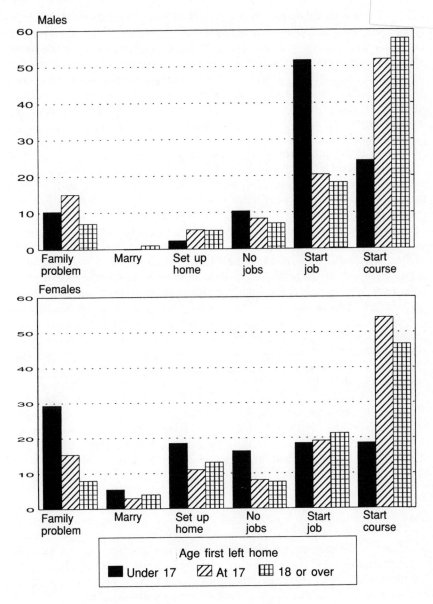

Source: SYPS 1987/89

'Traditional' reasons

These recent findings from the SYPS 1987/89 (Figure 3.1) show how the trends discussed in the previous chapter have continued over the last decade. Fewer young people now leave home by the age of 19 in order to form a partnership. This supports the idea that the link between leaving home and partnership formation is decreasing. According to the SYPS 1987/89, only 5 per cent of women leaving home by the age of 18 did so in order to marry, though rather higher numbers (19 per cent) reported leaving home 'to set up their own home' (which could have included partnership homes). Even if these two categories are combined, the proportions leaving home to live as married is considerably lower than that suggested by the NCDS data (Jones 1987a). Among the NCDS cohort, 32 per cent of women who had left home before the age of 18 said in 1981 that they had done so in order to 'live as married'. Further analysis comparing cohorts of the SYPS indicates, however, that while fewer women are leaving home by the age of 19 years in order to live with a partner, or to set up home, this might be becoming more common among men.

The 'scholastic' and 'professional' routes (Bloss *et al.* 1990) are, however, well represented in the SYPS data (Figure 3.1), and the extension of education is reflected in the higher proportions leaving home to go on a course, compared with 1981. Thus, among 16-year-old home-leavers, 24 per cent of men and 19 per cent of women left home in order to study (compared with 13 per cent of all who had left home by 18 years in the NCDS). Of those who left home at 17 or 18, about half have left in order to study. This finding is not surprising, given the extension of education and training in recent years. On the other hand, the proportions in the SYPS who left home at 16 years to take up a particular job were, at over 50 per cent among men and nearly 20 per cent among women, very similar to patterns in the NCDS for the under-18 age group. So, among 'traditional' reasons, marriage continues to decline, leaving home in order to study continues to increase, and leaving home to take up work remains, perhaps surprisingly, relatively stable.

'Problem' reasons

There are other reasons for leaving home which can be regarded as more problematic: because there were no jobs in the home area, and because of family conflict. Both these reasons indicate that leaving home was a matter of constraint, rather than a choice between two viable alternatives. Finally, leaving home for independence can also be classified as problematic, not because it necessarily reflects constraint, but because it may not be recognized as a legitimate reason for leaving. 'Problem' reasons for leaving home may therefore have their origins in the community and the family as well as the individual.

Lack of local opportunity
Some people indicated that they left home because there were no jobs in the area. This reason was more frequently given among those who left at 16 years, and decreased among later leavers, as other reasons become available. A recent study of homeless young Scots in London found that many had moved to London in the (unrealized) hope of finding work there (Shelter 1991).

Leaving home to look for work is particularly associated with the local economy (Furlong and Cooney 1990), and in Scotland lack of opportunities for study, training or employment in rural areas results in many young people leaving home in order to migrate to areas where such facilities exist. Young people from the remote rural areas of Scotland are, according to the SYPS, far more likely than young people in towns to have left their parental home by the age of 19 years (54 per cent compared with 32 per cent of those in other rural areas and only 25 per cent of those in towns), and are more likely to have migrated away from the home community. The young people studied (many of whom became migrants to towns) experienced problems on leaving home: they were more likely to miss their families than other groups, and the least likely to have left home because they did not get on with their parents (Jones 1990, 1992a). Their leaving home and migration away was associated with lack of local education and training opportunity; staying meant accepting the limitations of the local labour market (as MacDonald 1988, also found in a study of rural England). Eighty-one per cent of young Scots who stayed on in their rural areas were in the labour force, compared with 35 per cent of rural migrants to urban areas and 68 per cent of young people who grew up and stayed on in urban areas. Migrating away was mainly in order to study, a socially legitimate reason, nevertheless rural migrants to towns were more likely than young town-dwellers to experience problems in finding housing. The needs of young people in rural areas and the problems associated with rural deprivation continue to be overlooked.

Leaving home to look for work has become more difficult in recent years. The changes to the regulations for DSS board and lodgings allowances during the 1980s, after sensational reporting in the tabloid press about young people 'living it up on the Costa de Dole', meant that support for migration in search of work was gradually being withdrawn. Young people moving to towns from rural areas are now in a more difficult situation, and more reliant on family support. Some become homeless in towns (Shelter 1991), but rural homelessness has also become visible in recent years (Rural Development Commission 1992).

Family problems
Other reasons for leaving home can equally reflect constraint. The internal dynamics of family life can be adversely affected by social structural and spatial problems such as unemployment, and family breakdown can affect not only the relationship between parents, but also that between parents

and their children. Many young people left home because they did not get on with their families (Figure 3.1), and this was the main reason given by women who left home at 16 years of age (by 29 per cent of women and 10 per cent of men leaving home at this age). Proportions of women leaving for this reason decrease with age: 15 per cent of all 17-year-old leavers and only 8 per cent of 18-year-old leavers reported that they had left because of problems at home. These findings are similar to those from equivalent questions in the NCDS in 1981, where a category of 'negative reasons' (combining *'wanted to leave because of friction at home'*, *'was asked to leave because of friction at home'*, *'no longer allowed to stay there'* and *'accommodation poor'*) accounted for one-quarter of home-leaving before the age of 18. Those leaving home later were again more likely to leave for other reasons: only 12 per cent of men and 9 per cent of women leaving at 18 or 19 years left for 'negative' reasons (Jones 1987a).

Moving to independence

Increasing numbers of young people are leaving home in order to gain independence, as suggested in the previous chapter. This is a difficult concept to measure in a survey. Around 8 per cent of NCDS respondents who had left home said their main reason for leaving was to set up home (Jones, 1987a). This was relatively uncommon for men in the SYPS 1987/89, but 19 per cent of women who left home at 16 did so because they *'wanted to set up a home of (their) own'*.

Given the increasingly restricted opportunities young people in Britain have for obtaining employment, and even training places, the patterns may well continue to change. We saw in the last chapter that there has been an increase in proportions of young people returning home after leaving. Comparison of data from the SYPS 1987/89 with that of the SYPS 1989/91 (Jones 1993a:Figure 2.2) indicates that fewer people are now leaving home in order to look for work (perhaps because the risks were increased in 1988, with the removal of the social security safety net for those who do not find employment), while at the same time a higher proportion leave in order to start a course, continuing the trend. There is, however, no indication that leaving in order to take up a job has significantly decreased. Young workers are no less likely to leave home now than they were in 1989, or even in the late 1970s.

The nature of risk

If young people were really able to choose to leave home at the optimum time, they might leave home when they are older. It has been argued by some government ministers that young people should be encouraged to delay leaving home until they can afford to do so (or unless their families can afford to support them). It appears from these SYPS findings, though, that many young people have little choice in the timing of leaving home.

Table 3.1 Experience of homelessness by reason for leaving home and age at leaving, SYPS

	Proportion in each group who became homeless		
Reason for leaving	Left at 16/17 %	Left at 18/19 %	All %
'Traditional'	2	2	2
'Problem'	25	19	23
Independence	11	3	6
Other	10	5	7
All	7	4	5 (86)

Notes: 'Traditional' reasons include leaving in order to marry, study or take up a job. 'Problem' reasons include leaving because did not get on with family, or because there were no jobs in the area.
Source: SYPS 1989/91

Young people who leave home at 16 years of age are more likely to be leaving home because of problems at home, or because of the lack of local opportunities. In other words, rather than assume that the timing of entry into the housing market is a matter of individual choice and can be self- or family-regulated, we should consider those circumstances in which the possibilities for real, informed choice is limited and leaving becomes a matter of necessity.

The hypothesis that leaving home for 'problem' rather than 'traditional' reasons is more associated with risk in the housing market can now be tested. In general, there was relatively little overlap between the 'traditional' and 'problem' reasons given in the SYPS. People who left home in order to start a course or job or to marry tended not to report 'problem' reasons for leaving home as well. The survey data allow us to examine the most extreme risk in the housing market, that of homelessness. Table 3.1, based on the SYPS 1989/91, shows that 5 per cent of all who had left home had experienced homelessness (self-defined). However, 23 per cent of all those who left home for 'problem' reasons had been homeless since leaving home, compared with only 2 per cent of those who left home for 'traditional' reasons. Leaving in order to set up an independent home was not associated with risk of homelessness.

Age adds a further dimension, though, as suggested earlier. People who left home at ages 16 or 17 because of problems at home were more likely to have experienced homelessness than those who left for the same reason later (25 per cent, compared with 19 per cent). Risk therefore decreases with age, among those leaving home because of problems. This was not the case for those who left home for 'traditional' normative reasons, among whom age did not affect risk. However, the table also indicates that leaving home for independence is more risky for people under 18 years of age than it is for those aged over 18. These findings suggest that leaving home under the age of 18 should not be regarded as *per se* problematic. However, more housing provision and support is needed for young people who leave home under the age of 18 for 'problem' reasons. Their right to independent housing is not sufficiently recognized and they run a high risk of homelessness. Nevertheless, they have the least choice over the timing of their leaving home.

These findings thus support the hypothesis. Age at leaving home and reason for leaving home interact in the construction of risk. Homelessness is most likely to occur when people leave home in what has been constructed as 'the wrong way' and 'the wrong age'. These are social constructions which continue to develop and change. Unfortunately, they make it possible for normative and deviant behaviour to be so labelled, and for scapegoating of 'deviants' to occur. It is time to unpack the constructs, and to consider them in the context of choice and constraint.

Age is an important factor in determining risk in the housing market *when accompanied with other factors*. I would argue that the risk associated with age has its source in the structures of inequality rather than in the individual. There is, however, generalized concern about young people who leave the parental home 'prematurely'. There seem to be common assumptions about the levels of maturity associated with and expected of young people in their teenage years. The castigation of teenage mothers (effectively dispelled by Phoenix 1991) is based on assumptions that because of their age they are unable to provide adequate care, for example. As Hudson and Ineichen (1991) point out, teenage parenthood is not *per se* a problem and success depends on whether the right kind of help is available at the right time. Age-related myths are, however, reified in social policies and form the basis of a structure of age-grading in (for example) the benefit system and the legal system (as Jones and Wallace 1992, have argued). We should, however, take care to distinguish between the *legal* achievement of adulthood (which is closely tied to age) and the *social* achievement of adulthood (which is not).

Leaving home 'prematurely'?

It seems that the lower the age at which people leave home, the less likely their action to receive social approval or, therefore, social support. This includes parental support. Young's (1987) analysis showed that parents tended to regard their children's leaving home more favourably when it occurred either later or for marriage, job or study reasons, with a high proportion maintaining contact after their adult children had left home for these reasons. However, social support in broader terms is also withheld from young home-leavers, since government policies currently offer them little in the form of a safety net.

It is assumed that leaving home for a non-legitimated reason or at an age which does not carry a viable independent income is to leave home 'prematurely'. This can be applied to under-18s in particular, but also to anyone up to 25 years of age, when adult rates of benefit become payable. The term 'runaway' is indiscriminately applied (I take it to apply only to under-16s, and consider it even then to be an ill-advised label). Let us consider some of the difficulties associated with the notion of leaving 'prematurely'. The concept suggests:

- that young people should not leave home unless it is economically viable; this involves the application of an economic rationality model
- that leaving home is a matter of individual rational choice rather than structural constraint
- that leaving home is the result of discussion and negotiation between young people and their parents or guardians; this involves a model of domestic idyll and 'traditional' family values.

While there may be many young people to whom these criteria apply, there are others who cannot be expected to conform. Though Ermisch and Overton (1984) found an association between higher incomes and leaving home, for some young people, the economic viability of leaving may not be the priority consideration. It may not be economically viable for them to stay, if their parents cannot afford to keep them, or the home is over-crowded. Some may not be able to continue to live in their parental homes because they are being emotionally or physically damaged there. Young people leaving care have virtually no choice about when or how to leave.

Who are the 'early leavers'?

We have seen that overall, the middle class and women leave home earliest, while working-class men leave home last (Jones 1987a, 1990). Among the earliest home-leavers, however, are those who have to leave: to find work, or because of problems at home.

So who does leave home in their teenage years? The SYPS data was used in a multi-variate analysis to identify factors which could predict leaving home by the age of 19 years, either as independent effects, or in interaction with other variables (Jones 1993a). Variables were selected to reflect aspects of the individual, their family and their community. First, the number of siblings, father's economic status, whether they had a step-parent or lone parent, gave some indication of the family of origin. Next, the analysis took account of respondents' sex, the age at which they left school, whether they had truanted at school, their marital status, whether they had a child. Finally, the analysis included some indicators of local opportunity structures: whether they had ever had to move to a different town to find work, and their perception of the job opportunities in their area.

The analysis showed that not all these factors were significant, but some interacted in a complex way: large families (three or more siblings),

Table 3.2 Predicted values for leaving home by 19 years, SYPS

Characteristic	Prediction %	Standard error
Male	33	0.02
Female	40	0.01
Left school at 17 or over	41	0.01
Left school under 17	31	0.02
Married or cohabiting	68	0.04
Male	54	0.08
Female	77	0.03
Single	32	0.01
Male	30	0.01
Female	34	0.01
Step-parent at home	50	0.04
Male	55	0.07
Female	48	0.06
Both parents or lone parent	36	0.01
Male	31	0.02
Female	40	0.01

Note: Other factors associated with leaving home by the age of 19 were statistically significant in three-way interactions, including: family size; experience of unemployment; father not in full-time work; leaving school at 16 years.
Source: SYPS 1987/89

unemployment in the family, a young person's own unemployment, were associated with leaving home earlier – indicators of family disadvantage or poverty which appear to operate as push factors. Nevertheless, poverty in the home does not necessarily force a young person out: it is likely that where home circumstances are poor, young people will leave if they can afford to do so, but the economic factors which create or exacerbate problems at home may also make it impossible to leave. This is similar to the point made by De Jong Gierveld *et al.* (1991).

A simpler statistical model shows factors which could help predict whether someone had left home by the age of 19 years (Table 3.2). Factors with independent effects were: being female (40 per cent of females, compared with 33 per cent of males had left home), leaving school after the age of 17 years (41 per cent, compared with 31 per cent), being in a partnership (68 per cent, compared with 32 per cent) and having a step-parent (50 per cent, compared with 36 per cent). There are also some gender interactions, so that being male with a step-parent, and being female and married were both significantly associated with leaving home by the age of 19 years. In simple terms, leaving home by the age of 19 is most likely to occur among women, young people with partners, those with step-parents (in particular young men), and those with longer in education. Two of the most 'socially legitimated' reasons for leaving home – to form a partnership and to study – are thus represented here. The third main predictor of leaving home in the teenage years, having a step-parent, presents us with a new range of issues (see also Ainley 1991; Kiernan 1992).

Family breakdown/re-constitution

Many children have to cope with the breakdown of their parents' relationship. It has been suggested that, if present trends continue, 20 per cent of present day children will have experienced a parental divorce by the time they reach the age of 16 (Kiernan and Wicks 1990). This means that when young people are beginning to embark on adult life, increasing numbers of them are living with a lone parent or a step-parent. Some may have lost contact with one of their natural parents, while others may have had to re-negotiate their family relationships to allow the introduction of a step-parent and perhaps step-siblings. In these circumstances, there is enormous scope for family conflict. But conflict and stress in families can be associated with poor economic circumstances. There are higher divorce rates among families experiencing unemployment (Haskey 1984), and family breakdown can lead to the further poverty associated with lone parenthood. By extending the period of dependency of children on 'parents' (who may not in practice be their natural parents) and emphasizing parental responsibility, government policies have increased the potential for conflict within families (Maas 1986:12).

Parent-child relationships may have broken down before then, and the young person received into local authority care. The system for discharging young people from care and supporting their transition to independent living is woefully inadequate. They may be discharged from care with little preparation for independent living, and with no safeguards if they fail to compete in the outside world. Young people leaving care face a far higher than average risk of homelessness, as a result. Around a third of homeless young people have been in local authority care (Department of Environment 1981; Randall 1988; Liddiard and Hutson 1991a).

Over the last two decades, awareness has increased that some children suffer from physical and sexual abuse at the hands of their parents or other members of the parental household (see Hendessi, 1992, on homeless young people who have suffered abuse). This is often associated with other factors, such as marital breakdown, inadequate and overcrowded housing, and poverty. Some young people who leave home do so in order to protect themselves from further abuse. This questions the assumption that families can act as safety nets and provide shelter when the public sector and private markets fail.

We saw that being a step-child was one of the main predictive factors associated with leaving home by the age of 19 years. Young people with

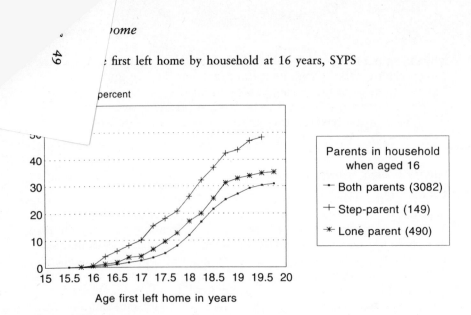

percent

Parents in household
when aged 16

-•- Both parents (3082)

-+- Step-parent (149)

-*- Lone parent (490)

Age first left home in years

Source: SYPS 1987/89

a step-parent (only around 4 per cent of the whole SYPS sample) are far
more likely than those with both natural parents or a lone parent to leave
home at 16 and 17 (Figure 3.2). By 19, 44 per cent of those with a step-
parent, compared with 33 per cent of those with a lone parent, and only
27 per cent of those with both parents, had left home. It is worth stressing
that, according to these findings, having a lone parent does not significantly affect the timing of leaving home. The reasons may be complex, but
the result is quite plain: step-children are disproportionately represented
among early home-leavers, as Ainley (1991), MORI (1991:xxiii–xxiv) and
Kiernan (1992) have also found.

When asked why they had left home, 40 per cent of step-daughters and
23 per cent of step-sons gave family problems as a reason, and among
step-daughters this was the reason most commonly given. In other words,
not only are step-children tending to leave home younger, but they are also
more likely to be leaving home for problem reasons. They are therefore a
'risk' group on both criteria. It is not surprising, then, that they are also
disproportionately found among homeless young people: 14 per cent of
SYPS respondents who had experienced homelessness had a step-parent at
16, compared with only 4 per cent of young people nationally. Our survey
of homeless young Scots similarly found that 13 per cent had a step-parent
at the age of 16, and at least one-quarter had a step-parent at the time of
interview, when their ages ranged from 16 to 22. This proportion increases
if such figures as 'mother's boyfriend' are included (see also Thornton
1990; Hutson and Liddiard 1991; Ainley 1991; Stockley *et al.* 1993).

Family dissolution and re-constitution appear to create serious problems for some young people. The SYPS follow-up interviews indicated, however, a range of experience which could result from family breakdown: it can involve gain as well as loss. While several young people did not get on with the step-parent, and this was a cause of family friction, in one case, the step-parent became an additional source of support. Family breakdown could result in the breaking off of relations with the departing parent's family, and the remaining family becoming closer and defended against the outside world (Jones 1995).

Family unemployment

The impact of family economic circumstances on patterns of leaving home is even more complex. Unemployment, indicating perhaps family poverty, may affect patterns of leaving home either by delaying it or by accelerating it. Previous research (Jones 1991) suggests that it may affect patterns of returning home, unemployed young people being twice as likely to return when their parents were employed. While the parents' economic status does not greatly affect the age at which people left home, it does seem to affect their reason for doing so. Young women left home because of family conflict mainly when their mothers were in full-time work and their fathers were not. Whether this is because of their fathers' presence in the home, or because in such circumstances daughters have to take on increased domestic responsibilities, or for other reasons, can only be conjectured. Young women with fathers not in full-time employment were also far less likely to leave home to go on a course and far more likely to leave home to set up their own homes (though not to marry) than those in families where fathers were in full-time employment (Jones 1993a).

Family unemployment appears, therefore, to contribute to risk in two ways: first, young people are more likely to leave home for problem reasons, and second, they are less likely to return home again. There may be an additional factor: that such families may not be able to provide financial support to young people leaving home (see Chapter 5).

Homeless young people

I have argued that while leaving home before the age of 18 years is not essentially problematic, it becomes so when the reasons for leaving are not perceived as legitimate. Homelessness was thus seen to occur mainly among early home-leavers who left home for 'problem' reasons. It is therefore not surprising that younger home-leavers and homeless young people have some characteristics in common, though earlier home leaving only leads to homelessness in a small minority of cases. The Homeless Survey, conducted by SCSH and CES in 1992 (see Appendix 2), provides data which are complementary to those in the SYPS, and we can therefore see why a larger sample of homeless young Scots first left their parental homes.

Figure 3.3 Reasons for first leaving home among 2 homeless samples, SYPS and Homeless Survey

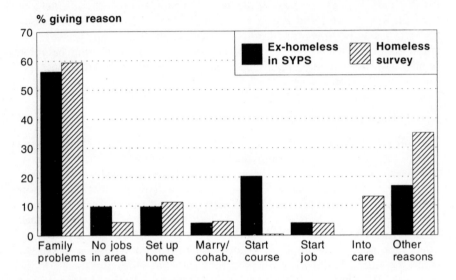

Note: SYPS 1991: all aged approx 19.25 years. Homeless Survey: ages 16–22 years.
Source: SYPS 1991; Homeless Survey

Overwhelmingly, homeless young people left home because they did not get on with the people there. Two sources give us the same finding: data from 86 respondents in the SYPS 1989/91 who had been homeless since leaving home, and data from the Homeless Survey of 246 currently homeless young people (Figure 3.3). In both cases family problems (*'didn't get on with the people at home'*) was the main reason given for first leaving home, by nearly 60 per cent in both groups. The main differences between the two groups, of ex-homeless and currently homeless, were that many of the ex-homeless in the SYPS had left home to start a course – this was very rare in the Homeless Survey. Thirteen per cent of those in the Homeless Survey had left home to go into care; this cannot be compared with the ex-homeless in the SYPS since the question was not asked of them.

Those who took part in the Homeless Survey were given the opportunity to write in other reasons, but these often became an elaboration of a pre-coded reason already given. Figure 3.4 shows that these tended to be associated with difficulties in family relationships, ranging from 'I got kicked out' (n = 17), to sexual or physical abuse of the young person (n = 13). In some cases, respondents blamed their parents, for drinking or nagging. In other cases, the respondents took the blame on themselves, reporting that they had been thrown out for taking drugs, gambling, 'doing daft things', or being out of control. Being unemployed was seen in this context.

Figure 3.4 Reasons for first leaving home, Homeless Survey

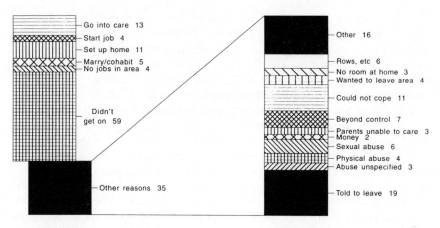

Pre-coded reasons (%)   Other reasons (n=)

Source: Homeless Survey 1992

Occasionally there were practical reasons, such as 'house getting over-crowded', or financial problems 'no money to pay rent to parents'. Many young people had not returned home since being received into local authority care, so the reasons for both were the same.

Around one-third of the respondents to the Homeless Survey had been in local authority care since the age of 14. Six said this was associated with truancy or their behaviour at school, and ten said they were beyond control. Sexual abuse was given as the reason in six cases and physical violence was an element in nine others – the latter not always on the part of a parent. Thus, one respondent said: 'I hit my mother because she treated me like dirt and didn't look after my gran properly', while another said they had been 'coming home drunk, fighting'. Violence at home may not have affected the young person directly: 'My mother was badly beaten up by my uncle and my mother was put in hospital'. Many of the written accounts indicate that the parental home was a place of danger rather than safety: parents' drink or drugs problems, their mental or physical health, may all be associated with neglect or abuse of their children. Family breakdown can take many forms, and does not necessarily involve the departure of a parent, though it may accelerate the departure of an adolescent child.

It is hard given these findings to suggest that these young people chose – in terms of free and informed choice – to leave home when they did. Rather, they may have had no other choice, and leaving home was a survival strategy for avoiding risk in the family home even though it meant facing new risks in the world outside.

Young people's constructions of legitimacy

Over and above the mainly quantitative data from the SYPS and the Homeless Survey, taped and transcribed in-depth interviews with a subset of 26 SYPS respondents provide vivid illustration and elaboration of the themes discussed so far. The interviews were conducted with a subset of SYPS respondents who fulfilled the 'risk' criteria identified through the above analysis: they had left home by the time they were 19 years of age, and they had not continued in education beyond the age of 16. Additionally, they came from families in which there was unemployment or families which had experienced marital breakdown (see Appendix 2 and Jones and Gilliland, 1993, for a fuller description of the sample). For a number of reasons, then, they had left home in difficult circumstances. One-third of this interview subset were found to have experienced homelessness and many had returned to live at home with their parents. They looked back at leaving home from their present circumstances at 21 years of age, with the benefit of hindsight. The interviews help to throw light on how people operate within a structure of constraint, their freedom to act as they would like, and the strategies they may use to optimize choice and maximize their resources. Further qualitative data from these interviews is presented in the following chapters, and three full biographies are given in Chapter 7.

The 'right way' to leave home

The interviews throw further light on the relationship between legitimacy and risk. It is striking that young people have a sense of the 'right' and 'wrong' ways of leaving home and have internalized some ideas about legitimate reasons for leaving, at least when they are looking back. Several referred to the 'right way' to leave home in a manner which corresponds to the above analysis. Some volunteered the information that the first time they left home it had been in the wrong way, and that next time they would 'do it right'. This would involve having an income and having a flat to go to. Leaving home on the spur of the moment was not seen as the appropriate way to leave, though many of them had done so first time round. Nevertheless, the issue of legitimation is not clear cut. Even leaving home because of a row can be associated with varying degrees of legitimation, as Eric's case indicates. He says that whether his parents helped him or not depended on the severity of the circumstances: 'It just depends how I was thrown oot – if I went oot with a big argument, really bad, or for something really bad, they wouldnae help me'.

Opportunities for leaving home for a legitimated reason are limited among younger home-leavers, since they are less likely to leave home in order to form a partnership or go on a course. Nevertheless, among the interview group, some, despite their age, appear to have been able to leave home in a legitimated way, and indeed with parental support. They are mainly young women who left home to live with partners. These include

Susan. Susan had a partner, a job and the opportunity of a flat, so thought 'why not' leave home, 'Give it a try, and if I don't like it, I'll go back home'. Nevertheless, she calls this a spur of the moment decision.

Some young women with children also appeared to have made a successful transition, with support. The complex relationship between having a child and getting independent housing (the subject of so much political debate currently) is brought out in the following extract from the interview with Jean (interviewer's words and comments in italic):

LG: What made you decide to leave home when you did?
J: I think it was because I had him [her child]. I wanted to get my ain house.
LG: Do you think that's a sort of natural thing to want?
J: Aye.
LG: Why?
J: I don't know ... I wouldn't have minded if I had to stay at my mum's, if I had no choice, but I thought 'Well, I've put my name down for a house'.
LG: If you hadn't had [child] would you have wanted to leave home?
J: No, I don't think so, no. Because you can't get a house, like, if you're single anyway. It usually takes about five years. The only way really to get a house of your own is if you've got a child, and if the house is too small, ... unless you bought one.

Having a child thus increased her housing chances and influenced her decision to leave home. Another respondent, Zoe, also says that if she had not been pregnant, she would not have been able to get housed and leave home. These accounts, while indicating that childbirth and housing are linked, do not suggest that either of these young women became pregnant in order to become housed; on the other hand they do suggest that having a child provides a legitimate reason for leaving the parental home.

Kenny and May both left for work-related reasons and with parental approval, but neither achieved a transition to independence, largely because of the nature of their work. They both moved into 'intermediate' surrogate households (see Chapters 2 and 6) in which their dependency was retained. Kenny left to join the army, and does not plan to leave home again until he has got into a good job with a steady income. May first left home with parental approval, to get a live-in job as a catering assistant at a private school, but she was given no freedom at all there and her father eventually took her away.

Many of those interviewed had a sense of the wrong and right ways to leave home, even though they did not necessarily practice what they now preach. Terry says, 'If I did it [left home again] I would do it right', so she is going to wait a few years until she is ready. 'Doing it right', for a teenager, would in Terry's view be leaving to get married or to go to college. It means leaving home in order to 'better' oneself, she says. Just moving out is in her view 'stupid'. Patricia, however, shows that there is many a slip! After returning home from her first attempt at leaving, she thought:

> P: I'm going to get a nice job and save up money and get a flat myself and start it all again, and do it the way I should have done it.
> *LG: So you came back here and you met your boyfriend?*
> P: Met my boyfriend and moved in wi' him!

She moved in with him gradually and justified this retrospectively:

> Then I just sort of gradually another day – added on another day, and then like in the next couple of months all my clothes were there and everything, and then there was no' really any point in coming home.

Back home again now, she wants to make another attempt to 'do it right' ('I mean I want to get engaged and get married and do it properly'), but there is still a slight hitch, because she and her boyfriend are about to spend the money they have saved for a deposit on a house on a holiday instead ('because I'll probably not get one for the next five or ten years').

With hindsight, most agreed in interview that planning is essential for success, but that planning is not always possible. For Axil, the 'right way' to leave home is to get housing first:

> A: Naewhere to go, that's it. Naewhere to go, you cannae go.
> *LG: What about your furniture?*
> A: Worry aboot that later. I just worry aboot getting a hoose first.

For Joe, Sandra and Chris, on the other hand, the 'right way' would be to get a job first, though now Sandra thinks she would rather leave home to get married. Jai says he would need a steady income and also indicates that leaving the 'right way' means discussing it with your parents. Now that her father has died, May would only be able to leave home without guilt if she gave her mother plenty of warning, but even then it would be difficult. Peter now says planning is essential (he also says that people should leave home because it is the *right thing for them*, and not because they are fighting their parents, or 'fitting in wi' the cliché').

Jill points out (and we shall see later in this book that she could well be right) that no 16-year-old could afford to live in a house on their own, 'Unless they had a really good job, or they were moving in with somebody that had a really good job, I would say they're wasting their time. I mean they might go, but they would probably be back [home] in 6 months' time.' Later, she reflects,

> I'm happy enough because I've never had nae real downfall, but if I started again I'd probably have stayed at home longer, or I would have gone out and bought a flat – or got my own flat. I wouldn't have messed aboot biding with so-and-so, and flitting in wi' so-and-so. I would have made sure it was my house.

Some interviewees stressed the legitimacy of their first moves away from home, despite their age. Rosco points out that 'it made sense' on the grounds of convenience to leave home when he did. Thus also, Shona says that she left home because it was convenient for her work: 'It was handier the way it worked out, but in a way I wish I didn't have to leave that way, you know'.

Other people (especially her father, who did not want to lose his only daughter) did not approve of her leaving at 16, though: 'You don't leave home when you're 16, kind of thing. They just didn't like it, a lot of them.' Jai says that leaving home when he did, ahead of his friends, made him into 'something of a cult hero'.

Leaving home for non-legitimated reasons

Like many other younger home-leavers and homeless young people, several of the SYPS case study interviewees left home following or during rows with their parents, and may have had nowhere planned to go to. Retrospectively, they too may justify their actions, and even the actions of their parents in evicting them. Given earlier findings, either of these reasons may be associated with risk, especially among this age group. Some had little choice about the way they left home, but were told to leave: Eric, Joe from his mum's, Janice, Charlie. Sean now justifies his mother's action in sending him to live with his father (whom he did not know) as legitimate, even though at the time he pleaded to be allowed to stay:

> She regrets doing it but – 'don't you think it's the best thing, what had happened at that point in time?' and in retrospect obviously I do. I don't know what I would have done if I'd ... stayed at school.

Denise left home when she was 14 'because anything was better than that. I couldnae handle it.' She justifies her leaving home in terms of her mother's behaviour.

Others are unable to leave home because they cannot justify doing so. May could not leave home when her father was ill and she was made to feel guilty about wanting to leave (she even had a flat arranged). Zoe's parents did not want her to leave, and tried to keep her in all sorts of ways (including by offering to build an extension to the house). The only way she was able to leave home was because she had a baby, which in a sense legitimized her leaving. Jai now regrets that the manner of his leaving home was hurtful to his mother.

Retrospective justification tends, however, to hide the pain that may have been involved in the initial leaving. Parents tend not to 'ask' their children to leave: they tell them. Eric talks of the endless rows with his mother and their consequences:

> E: She started saying 'Right, get oot, get oot,' and started roaring at me, and roaring at me. And I'd just start roaring and shouting back at her.

LG: *And how did she get you out?*

E: I would go.

LG: *Did you just walk out?*

E: Aye. Aye. I wouldnae sit doon and say 'I'm not going.' I would just go.

Janice's rows with her mother were in a similar mould:

J: When I say arguing, it just wasnae shouting and bawling, it was like battering each other and kicking lumps off each other – that sort of thing. And she just like told me to go and I just wasnae going to stay there wi' her going on like that.

LG: *Did you pack your bags and go?*

J: I just put everything, all my clothes in like a big red bin bag it wis, and I just took that frae place to place.

LG: *So you didn't know where you were going when you left?*

J: No. I just went to a friend's and stayed there for a while, then just kept kind of moving on.

Janice and Eric were not physically thrown out of the house, nor were they asked to leave: they were put in a position where they felt there was no alternative but to go, whatever the consequences.

Independence and risk

The interviews also throw light on what young people mean by independence, and the extent to which they feel they can achieve independence by leaving home. Leaving home was frequently seen as a means of growing up, rather than as a consequence of it. Several young people described how their relationships with their parents improved when they left home, since they began to treat them as adults. For some, adult independence means emancipation from parental control as well as 'standing on your own two feet' in economic terms, and the two may go hand in hand. It is a complex issue for young people. Those with employment appear to be able to live in the parental home, and earn a degree of emancipation from dependency by paying their keep (see Chapter 4). Those without employment tend on the other hand to equate independence with leaving home. Often, though, the lines are blurred.

The quotations above suggest that with hindsight young people may see home-leaving as consequent on successful transition into the labour market, rather than parallel with it, but perhaps this economic rationality is only possible with hindsight.

Many of these young people say they have grown up and learned through the experience of leaving home, even though this involved risks. These were perceived by them to be positive and necessary. Sometimes, they acted out of curiosity. Susan left home to live alone in a flat owned by her father:

LG: What made you decide to leave home at 17?
S: I don't know. Probably just my independence. Try and see what it was like really. I mean, none of my friends were planning on moving out or anything. They were quite shocked that I sort of packed all my stuff and went to my dad's flat. But I'm glad that I did it.

Whatever the risk, young people may leave home as a means of testing and hopefully proving their ability to be independent individuals. This is much more than just living independently. It is an assertion of their identity, if it works. By taking risks some could prove to their parents that they could cope. Thus Terry says that when she left home, her parents were apprehensive, but now they have more faith in her ability to live independently. And asked by his parents if he was sure he was doing the right thing, Kevin replied: 'You don't know till you try . . . You just have tae wait and see if it works oot or not'.

Amy was excited by the newness of her experience moving into a flat on her own 'that feeling that everything's new, you're in a strange place . . . and even going down to the shops was an excitement!'. She wishes her family had forced her to stand on her own two feet, as it was a shock when she moved, and besides, she is frightened of being on her own. She says you have to act 'rather than dwell on the thought and start to regret it',

> I think I just said to myself, 'You've got to [cope].' Either that or you crack up. Or you move back into your parent's house. There's no' really a medium you can go. You've either just got to move back or get on with it.

Learning from mistakes

It is part of a young person's concern to be able to take responsibility for their own lives – an important aspect of adult independence – that leads them to take risks. Learning from mistakes is a common theme in the interviews. May says that people learn by their mistakes: 'it's just something you've just got to learn by yourself'. Jill says her life has been 'shitty' but 'that's through my fault.' She says that she was not old enough at 16 to live independently, and if she started again, she would have stayed at home longer. Obviously, she says, she was not ready:

> . . . obviously I wasnae or I wouldn't have made the mistakes I made. But there was no good anybody had sat me down and said 'You're no' ready to leave home', because I was convinced I was.

For Patricia, the opportunity to take risks was important even if she was likely to make mistakes. In retrospect she thinks that leaving home when she did was the worst mistake she ever made, though as in Jill's case there was no stopping her at the time. She wanted freedom:

> I wanted just a bit of freedom so that I could make my own choice. But my choices were getting made for me, so I wanted to say 'Right.

OK, I'll make that decision.' And most of the time it was the wrong decision, and I learned from my mistakes, but if I could make that mistake myself that was fine. It was my mistake. I made it.

Peter cannot understand his contemporaries who are still 'apron-stringed up' to their parents (though he himself was homesick when he left). He first left home because he felt independent:

It's just a challenge you've got to accept. It's just adding that wee bit mair experience tae yer life. In a way, I suppose that is growing up. The mair experience you gain, the mair of an adult you become.

And he was pleased to come back and show how he had changed, 'Look. This is me. I am a person.' The next time he left 'they were higher risks', he says, because 'I could have failed easier the second time around'. Back home now, he is more cautious: 'I wid prepare if I was ever gonna leave home again. I would definitely prepare. I would leave nothing to chance, because it can deal you bad deals all the time.'

As Peter indicates, once having failed, young people need good reason to take the same risk again. Polly had two chances of council flats, but did not take them up because she was not ready to move out. Jai is currently weighing up the risk of leaving home, at a time when his small business is just being set up and his income is uncertain: 'I'd just need to cover myself for everything that could possibly go wrong', but when he first left home when he was quite young, he just thought 'I'll give it a try'. He says he learnt from the experiences he had.

These qualitative data show how important it is that young people should be supported in their transition to adulthood. They are trying to become independent adults, and will resist attempts to keep them in the position of dependent children, 'apron-stringed' to their parents.

Structure and agency

This chapter has examined the extent to which young people's patterns of leaving home are determined by extended opportunities (for instance to study) and increased constraints (lack of adequate incomes, supportive family life and affordable housing), and how in the face of these structures of opportunity and inequality, they seek to forge their own biographies. In consequence, they encounter increased risk.

In thinking about the extent to which young people act according to their own volition and the extent to which their behaviour is a response to constraint, we can begin to face another question. Is entry into the housing market regulated by young people, their families, or by the state (as education, training, employment, social security and other government policies seem to intend)? The answer seems crucial, because as indicated earlier, the two sides in the debate about youth housing and homelessness take opposing views on whether housing supply should be extended or demand reduced. This chapter suggests, however, that in so far as leaving home creates a housing demand, then demand cannot easily be regulated. With increasing family breakdown, and more complex family relationships, regulation by the family becomes more difficult. State regulation appears only to increase risk, rather than change the pattern of leaving home. The extension of education means not only that more people leave home to study, but that more non-students see leaving home in the teenage years as a model of independence for which they too should strive. The withdrawal of state support for leaving home runs counter to this move towards attempted self-determination.

Unlike the age at leaving compulsory education, which is fixed by education policies, there is no 'correct' age at which leaving home becomes statutorily recognized. The notion that some young people leave prematurely while others delay their departure is part of an attempt to impose a norm on behaviour which, as we have seen, does not easily fit into this framework. Yet, age affects risk, not because of the characteristics of the young person leaving home, but because of the social structures they enter on leaving home – structures of social security and the labour market which tend increasingly to discriminate against the young.

In some respects it is worrying that young people need to take responsibility for what they perceive as their own mistakes, since there may be circumstances in which their only mistake was to misread, or be overly optimistic about, an ever-decreasing opportunity structure. Thus, the jobless or the homeless may blame themselves for faults which really lie with the labour or housing markets. In other words, their need to feel responsible for themselves and emancipated from external control makes them ideal fodder for those who prefer to deny the state's responsibilities and to consider the homeless and jobless as a self-perpetuating and deviant underclass.

Chapter 4
Returning home

Leaving home in the late twentieth century is often only one stage in a process which eventually leads to household formation and independent housing. This process can take several years, involving two or more leaving home events. Many young people move into transitional intermediate households, from where they may either move on into independent households of their own, or return to the family home again. The transition out of the family home is thus a complex process which can be reversible, involving returns as well as departures. In the last chapter we saw how leaving home requires justification and legitimation, this is also the case with returning home. And as with leaving home, returning may be an outcome of constraint rather than choice. These issues will be explored. We shall see that returning home can involve a return to childlike dependence which many young people will resist or reject, but also that ultimately the initiative for a return home may lie not with the young person but with their parent. Finally, the implications of not being able to return home will be considered, and the idea that the family home can provide a safe haven for the potentially homeless will be explored further.

While more young people have left home by the age of 19, the proportion returning has doubled in recent years (Figure 2.1). This chapter will indicate why this might be, and also its implications. Let us first identify the practice of returning home within the process of leaving. In the research reported, returns home were for significant periods of time, usually six months, and thus excluded brief visits or stays during holidays. On the basis of her Australian research, Young suggests that the incidence of returning home peaks during the second year away from home, and is generally completed within five years of first leaving. Her analysis (1987:19) indicates that: 'the major part of the movement from home and back again is completed by age 25 years, and beyond that age the adult child has finally established independent and permanent living arrangements away from the parents' household'. The whole process of leaving the parental home and establishing an independent one can thus take several years of young adulthood. By keeping open the option of returning home, parents can offer one means of supporting the transition to independence, providing a secure base from which to become independent or a safety net for those who may need one. Not all do this, however, and we shall discover that there are problems surrounding the right of young people to return home once they have left it.

Patterns of returning home are changing because of the changing patterns of leaving home. Young suggests that one reason why returning home has become more common is because fewer people leave home in order to marry. Returns to the parental home mostly occur when people leave for non-marital reasons, and the practice is therefore most common among men and younger leavers (Young 1984). Forty-four per cent of men and 37 per cent of women in her study returned home after leaving (Young 1987:Table 4.1). Both later first-time leavers, and returners who were leaving for a second time, were more likely to be leaving home in order to marry and less likely to return again. Among the others, it was not uncommon that returning home would be part of an extended process of household formation.

Evidence of patterns of returning home in Britain exists in the NCDS, and shows social class and gender differences. At the age of 23, 47 per cent of men and 25 per cent of women were living with their parents, but of these, 30 per cent of men and 38 per cent of women had previously left home for a period of six months or more. Women are thus more likely to have left and (among leavers) more likely to have returned. There were also social class differences: returning home was mainly associated with the middle class of both sexes. Returning home varies with reason for leaving, and as Young found, returning was least associated with leaving in order to live as married (Jones 1987a). The disparity with the Australian findings may occur because the NCDS analysis only covered young people up to the age of 23 years. Among all those who had left home, 29 per cent had returned home for six months or more, proportions varying according to the reason they left (Table 4.1). The findings support the idea that returning home is least associated with leaving for the most traditional reason of marriage, and most associated with leaving in order to study or take up a job.

Although leaving home is part of an overall process of becoming adult, and is therefore usually inevitable, it seems that people still need a good reason to leave (the last chapter suggested that support for setting up home may depend on the legitimacy ascribed to the reason for leaving home). Those who leave home in order to start a particular course, or a particular job, or to live with a partner, may return home when the course ends, or the job finishes, or – less commonly – when the partnership breaks up

Table 4.1 Returning home by reason for leaving, NCDS

Reason for leaving	Returned %
To live as married	11
To set up on own	27
For 'problem' reasons	45
To begin studies	48
To take up a job	52
All	29

Source: NCDS 1981

(Rauta 1986). This is supported by findings described below. It would indicate that in some circumstances, once the legitimate reasons for being away from home no longer exist, a return home may be an expected option, and another reason will be needed for another move away. Young's research indicates that the reason for leaving the second time tends to be more 'traditional' and thus legitimated. Returning home may thus provide an opportunity to repair a previous action perceived as a wrong-doing.

The problem reasons identified in Table 4.1 were: wanting to leave or being asked to leave because of friction at home, no longer allowed to stay at home, and poor accommodation. It is mainly the younger leavers who leave for 'problem' reasons as we saw in the last chapter. According to the NCDS 1981, 45 per cent of those who left home for these 'problem reasons' had returned home again.

If, as Young indicates, most returns home are completed by the age of 25 years, then the NCDS data on 23-year-olds provide a partial picture of returners. A sample of 25-year-olds who had left home and returned might, for example, include more who had left for marital reasons and returned because their partnerships had split up. The SYPS data discussed below gives evidence of returning home among earlier leavers.

Leaving home and living away

The distinction between 'leaving home' and 'living away' from home becomes particularly useful here (Leonard 1980). 'Living away' from home keeps open the option of returning, while 'leaving home' is more likely to constitute a definite break. The question arises whether living away from home constitutes a move to independence and emancipation from parental authority (and its corollary, parental support). Just as in nineteenth-century Britain leaving the parental household was associated with entering a surrogate family household ('intermediate household') for a number of years before formation of a new family household independent of the family of origin, so it appears that the present-day gradual process of leaving home often includes a period in transitional housing, in intermediate households, before household formation is achieved. This intermediate household and housing situation reflects the intermediate stage of semi-independence through which young people move between childhood dependence and adult independence. Whether this is appropriate or desirable is another issue. The fact is that it happens. Living away from home is a part of a weaning process, not the result of one.

'Living away' from the parental home is thus a useful concept since it indicates that the leaving home event can be reversed. It is most commonly associated with students in higher education, who may return home in the vacations or at the end of their course, and to whom 'home' may still mean the parental home, rather than their term-time address. Young's two studies (1974, 1984), the first based on mothers' answers to questions about when their children left home, and the second based on questions asked of the young adults themselves, shows how confusion can occur. Parental and children's definitions are clearly likely to vary, as are expectations about whether leaving home is permanent or temporary, and young people were found by Young to be more likely than their parents to report the full extent of leaving and returning. However complex the study of the process of leaving home has become, it seems though that returning home has become more common, and the leaving home process more reversible, across a wider section of society. The result is that returning home is no longer the province of students.

We saw in Chapter 2 that the proportions returning home have increased in recent years. Twenty-eight per cent of those who had left home had returned to their parental homes again by the time they were surveyed in 1991 at the age of 19 years (see Figure 2.1). The implications of extending what appears to have been an essentially middle-class practice to young people from working-class backgrounds will be discussed below. Working class transitions out of the parental home were typically for marriage, were less likely to involve transitional households, and were less likely to be reversible.

Choice or constraint?

As with patterns of leaving home, it is, however, difficult to determine whether returning home is a matter of choice or a response to constraint, and there are grounds for expecting social class differences in this respect. Many young people do return home: this may be because it is convenient for them to do so, because they have missed their families, because the reason they left has passed, or because they decide the time is not yet right for them to make the final break from the parental home.

The SYPS 1985/6/7 included questions about the problems young people had when they left home. It is a pity that they were not also asked about the advantages of leaving home. As a result we may get a skewed picture, but the fact that the question was missing reflects a societal concern that leaving home in the teenage years was somehow essentially problematic. Many young Scots appear to have found it emotionally difficult to leave home, saying that they missed their families or their friends (Jones 1990:35). This was particularly the case where migration had occurred. Those reporting missing their families or friends tended to be those who left home to start work, to look for work, or to study, rather than those who left because of family problems or to set up home. The emotive aspects of leaving home are therefore reflected here. However, many also experienced practical and financial problems when they left home. The main problem of this sort was related to money and bills, but 42 per cent of those leaving home to look for work elsewhere reported problems finding housing, as did 34 per cent of those who left home because of family problems. This is important in the light of a later finding, reported below, that these are the groups most likely to return to the parental home. Earlier leavers who left to start work are more likely to move into housing which is connected with their job (Jones 1990).

So returning home could be a response to emotional, practical or financial need, and it could mean a transition deferred. In some circumstances, the initial move away from the parental home may have been conceived as temporary. It is interesting then that having housing problems was not particularly associated with returning home (Jones 1990:37).

Who returns to the parental home?

Just as early leavers were identified in the last chapter, so early 'returners' in the SYPS can be identified here (Table 4.2). Some of these young people were affected by the 1988 changes in social security regulations, and would have been in theory or in practice forced into a resumption of dependence or semi-dependence on their parents. The group most likely to have returned home by the age of 19 were those who had originally left home to look for work, and this could be a direct outcome of the withdrawal of their right to social security. Though leaving home to look for work was not common, except among younger leavers (as Figure 3.1 showed), it is associated with migration away from the home community. Analysis of an earlier SYPS cohort found that 44 per cent of returners, compared with only 33 per cent of leavers, reported having moved town to look for work (Jones 1990). The indications are that young migrants looking for work may be forced to return home if they do not find it.

These findings are not dissimilar from those in the NCDS when the age factor is taken into account. By surveying at the age of 19, we lose a lot of the pattern of returning home, which may take place over the next few years. However, Young indicates that younger home leavers leaving for non-marital reasons are those most likely to return home. It is likely that many of those who left to go on a course will return, but 19 is too young

Table 4.2 Reasons given for leaving and returning, SYPS

Reason for leaving	%	Sign. p = <
Problems at home (44% returned)		
Family wanted me back	41	.000
Financial reasons	34	.000
More convenient	28	.005
Couldn't find anywhere to live	23	.000
Didn't get on with flatmates	14	.000
Partnership broke up	10	.05
Job finished	5	.01
Wanted to set up own home (18% returned)		
Financial reasons	50	.000
Didn't get on with flatmates	41	.000
Family wanted me back	41	.000
More convenient	36	.05
Became unemployed	23	.01
Partnership broke up	18	.005
Looking for work (65% returned)		
Only left temporarily	56	.005
Lonely	17	.05
Starting a particular job (38% returned)		
Job finished	48	.000
Became unemployed	14	.005
Financial reasons	11	.05
Starting a course (16% returned)		
Course finished	50	.000
Only left temporarily	27	.05
Family wanted me back	5	.001
Getting married (13% returned)		
Partnership broke up	43	.000

Note: Reasons for returning home (indented), by reasons given for leaving (in bold), among those who have ever left and returned (n = 411).
Source: SYPS 1989/91

an age to show this as the respondents would still be on their courses. Of those who left home to start a particular job, 38% returned by the age of 19. Leaving home for 'problem' reasons (family conflict, or because there were no jobs locally) appears to be more closely associated with returns home: of those who left home because of problems at home, 44 per cent returned home, while of those who left in order to look for work, as many as 65 per cent returned. Given that this group are those most likely also to have had housing problems on leaving home, and even to have faced homelessness, we should consider whether returning home is a strategy which can prevent homelessness (see also Chapter 6).

We asked returners to give the reasons why they had returned home (Table 4.2). There is a close connection between the reason for leaving and the reason for returning in many cases. This may make returning home easier to justify. Notably, leaving to start a course, job, or partnership are mainly associated with returning because the course, job or partnership ended. Some of those who left home to look for work, take up a job, or start a course pointed out that they had only left home temporarily, in any case. Of those who left home because of problems at home, and who later returned, the main reason for returning was that their families 'wanted them back' (41 per cent of them gave this reason for returning). This finding will be seen to be important when the qualitative data on returning home are examined below. The survey findings thus provide an important clue to the problem of access to the family home, when the right to live there does not necessarily exist.

Some people returned because they had experienced specific problems living away from home. They had not necessarily 'only left home temporarily', but they may have been forced to return. There are indications of problems finding housing or financial problems, which mainly affected those who left to set up their own homes or because of family problems. Of those who left home because of family problems, 23 per cent returned because they could not find anywhere to live, and 34 per cent of them said they had returned because of financial problems. Finally, leaving home for independence reasons (*wanted to set up own home*) was not particularly associated with returning home again and only 18 per cent returned. Among those that did return, 50 per cent had financial problems. It seems that some had attempted flat sharing, because 41 per cent of those who had left for independence returned because they did not get on with their flatmates.

Whatever the reason for returning home, there may be problems with doing so. While young people who have been living away, and who only left temporarily, may have relatively easy access to the family home, this may be more difficult in situations where the young person and their families saw the departure from home as a definite break. In circumstances where the young person leaves home because of conflict, a return home may be even more difficult. We shall see that some complex negotiations may have to take place.

Ambivalence

Young people may be ambivalent about whether or not to live in the parental home, and whether or not to return there. The ambivalence (about whether or not to let them) may extend to their parents too. This makes it difficult to determine whether they choose to leave or return, or whether these actions reflect constraint. Opportunities for young people to establish an independent home have been reduced, but then with increased family breakdown and family poverty, so might opportunities to stay at home.

It would be wrong to assume that young people living with their families are necessarily constrained to live there and in practice 'hidden homeless' (viz Rauta 1986), or that formal support and housing provision outside the family is necessarily the ideal. Theories of economic rationality do not explain all leaving home behaviour: young people who have the means to set up independent homes may remain in their parental homes, just as those without the means may leave. Families often act as caring environments within which transitions to adulthood can be effected, and emancipation can perhaps be achieved within the family home. The pattern according to which working-class males tend to stay longest in the parental home may reflect their desire to have their needs catered for by their mothers until the role can be taken on by their wives (Wallace 1987; Rauta 1986). A young person with a chronic illness or disability may be more appropriately cared for within their family than in the outside world. It may, too, be helpful to a young mother to live with her own parents, so long as their relationship is good, and the situation offers support and a degree of independence and privacy. In other circumstances, though, given decent accommodation, a realistic income and good child care facilities, the same young mother might be better off living independently, but these other circumstances do not commonly prevail. Burton *et al.* (1989:9) warn that: 'The apparently positive attitudes of many young people towards living with their family is difficult to disentangle from the recognition that there are few economically viable alternatives'. Commentators thus warn of the dangers of superficial assessment. Emmanuel (1987:32, quoted in Burton *et al.* 1989) makes the point that in Greece:

> Living with the family and, more generally, being dependent on family support is part of the whole network of family relationships and the mutual obligations involved. It has obvious benefits as well as costs for the young ... There are a lot of people that would react violently to any idea of replacing the main functions of this system with social welfare apparatus or, for the more well-off, a friendly bank manager.

It is one of the principal roles of parents to help their children grow into independent adults, but this can be fraught with difficulty. There may be ambivalence on both sides: parents may have an interest in keeping their children dependent on them and at home, rather than lose them, and young people may in part enjoy the comforts of home and being mothered (if their experience of childhood has been positive). There is thus a multi-faceted problem. These issues will be explored with data from the SYPS case studies. We have no data here on the experience of parents. As far as young people are concerned, they are having to deal with the ambivalence of their semi-dependent and semi-independent status, as well as negotiate with their parents. In practice it seems that parents employ strategies of control and their children employ counter-strategies of resistance, until, as a result of further re-negotiation and emancipation of the young person, a more reciprocal and equal relationship can be achieved.

The problem of dependency

Returning home, at a time when a young person is attempting to be independent, involves backtracking along the transition path, and in many cases a return to childlike dependency: 'So I just came back here and it was all secure again. I was in my mum's arms. I felt dead good' (Patricia). This return to dependency presents new problems, as we shall see, and the safety net of the family home may not always be appreciated, if it provides too easy an option. Amy says she wishes her parents would push her out and say 'You're not coming back. That's it', because she feels too protected.

Diana Leonard (1980) found that parents may spoil their young in order to maintain dependency and closeness. While this was also found in our Scottish study, it was not always a successful strategy. Though young people enjoy home comforts when everything is done for them, they also rebel against it. It was particularly the young men who tended to like being looked after and young women who tended towards resistance. Joe liked living at his granny's, because she used to run his baths and 'bring me a fry and a' that in the morning', and Axil stays at home because 'I ken where my bread's buttered'. Jai says 'I've got my feet under the table again', and comments that when he returned home: 'My mum was well chuffed – "my wee baby!" '. Peter, though, is 'freaked out' that his friends have not left home, and thinks 'Haven't you got a life, man? Are you gonna be still apron-stringed?'.

Too much, and too extended, mothering had a disempowering effect on some, making most of the young women feel lazy about growing up and learning to become independent. Thus Jean did not want to leave home because everything was being done for her there ('I was getting it too good at my mum's!'). As a result, she was ill-prepared for leaving home. Amy similarly never had to contribute to anything at home, 'so when I moved oot it was a shock'. Janet, however, says:

> We were all brought up to stand on oor ain two feet. We werenae brought up to hide behind my ma's apron strings ... There's nae point in wrapping ye up in cotton wool, because let's face it, ye're gonna go oot in the world, you're gonna go oot there and fend for yourself, so it is better knowing how to get by a wee bit.

When Amy later returned home, she enjoyed it at first ('the first couple of weeks it was too much of a novelty to be back') but soon became worried that she was 'getting too used to being dependent on them again', and moved out for a second time.

Young people may resist dependence through rejecting parental support or through re-defining it in some way. Some may not return home at all, rather than resume their dependence. Several who had returned home reacted against 'home comforts', as Amy did. The previous chapter indicated how some young people felt they had grown up through leaving home, and had thus achieved a greater degree of equality with their parents. Moving back would in these terms mean a resumption of childlike dependency and signify failure, but this is not always the case.

Even while living with their parents, young people feel they can achieve a degree of independence and emancipation by paying for their keep. This may present a cheap housing option for those who want to and can stay at home, and we shall see in Chapter 6 how 'dig money' compares with the housing costs of those who have left home. Dig money is not covered by training allowances (currently £29.50 in the first year and £35 in the second), and it has been suggested that young people living in the parental home have no housing costs, but can live at the expense of their parents. Thus, Robert Jackson, MP, stated in a parliamentary reply about the training allowance: 'We believe that the existing minimal levels are sufficient to meet the normal requirements of a young person living in the parental home' (Hansard, 18 February 1992, quoted in Maclagan 1992). Earlier research (Jones 1991) has shown that this is not the case. Nearly all young people who have left full-time education pay board, whether they are working, on schemes or unemployed, and the level of payment corresponds as much to the financial circumstances of the parents as to those of the child. Thus, young people on training allowances pay almost as much as their peers in other circumstances, but in their case this may represent most of their income, leaving them with little scope to save or to spend.

Those interviewed speak about the obligation to pay dig money, even if they can ill afford it. Payments into the household economy form one element in the complex pattern of economic and indeed social relationships. They may constitute the justification for remaining in the parental home, and allow those who do remain to retain a degree of independence and a way to avoid feeling spoilt. Amy was aware that she was an exception among the case studies. She was never asked for money for staying at home, though 'we had our chores and that', and she remarks later 'my mum and dad were *a bit wrong* in the attitude they had. They never took any money off us.'

Those living at home or with relatives were occasionally getting subsidized by them, through paying a reduced level of board money. Shona was thus able to save money by living at home:

The thing was, before I had my daughter, like I was able to save up some money, whereas I wouldn't have been able to. That was one thing, I wouldn't have ever been able to save up so much money as what I did, and I would have been flat broke, not been able to buy anything.

Outside the immediate family, expectations varied considerably. Joe, when living with a relative of his girlfriend, paid less than other residents 'she wasnae taking the right amount off me than she took off lodgers', but this was not the general rule: Amy says that her aunt would have evicted her if she had not paid the rent ('business is business', she says).

In Sandra's family, dig money formed an important part of the household economy ('she's got the three of us wi' dig money'), and Sandra also pays money into the household budget in other ways. Peter's comments show how the payment of dig money can confer a degree of emancipation: 'I was paying digs – that's what's *required of you* when you're in the hoose ... I'll do what I want, no' what you want. I pay my digs here and that is it.' Dig money formed part of his obligation to his parents. But the obligation is mutual. He says he gives what he can and a wee bit extra sometimes to help them out. When he was unemployed, they took less off him 'but then again, is that no' *what parents are supposed tae dae*.' Jai's parents sometimes help him out in this way. He is trying to set up a business: he says he should be paying his parents £30 a week, but last week could only pay them £5. Jill explains that when she first had her baby and was living at home, she could not have paid board because she would have had nothing left 'so like when I stayed with my mum she like kept me'. The setting of dig money levels, therefore, relates to mutual understandings of obligation.

A parent can also abuse the situation: when she was living at home, Janice paid her mother £15 dig money, but 'she was always tapping money off me when I just started working', and didn't give it back. Her mother wanted her to pay more: 'I know that £15 dig money isnae a lot when you're running a house, things like that, but *I'm her daughter*'. Janice now receives dig money of about £5 from her sister, who has left home and lives with her, but she is putting it by for her. This is a pattern commented on in Brannen *et al.* (1994).

The ambivalence of many young people wanting both independence and the comforts of home will be further evidenced below. For many young people, the first entry into the housing market may be tentative – a personal testing out – and their presence in the market only temporary. They may subsequently decide to wait before trying again, either because they are in no hurry to take on the responsibilities of independent living, or because they cannot afford to do so.

The problem of claiming the right to return

A young person who is not in full-time education cannot easily claim a right to return home and live as licensee of their parents, when there is no legal obligation for their parents to provide a home. Provision of a home is one of the main forms of support which parents can offer a young person. It can provide a safety net if independent living becomes difficult.

The indications are that while leaving home for a legitimated reason tends to leave the door of the family home ajar, so that returns home can be effected, leaving home for a non-legitimated reason makes a return home more difficult. The potential for the family home to act as a safety net, if independent living becomes too difficult, thus varies considerably. In these cases, an invitation to return home becomes important.

The interviews with the SYPS subset, one-third of whom had experienced homelessness, shows how returns home were effected in practice. Two criteria were found to be important: whether an invitation to return (whether explicit or not) existed at the time a young person left home, or whether an invitation was subsequently given. An indication that this might be important was revealed in the survey finding described above. The alternative scenario would involve young people having to ask if they could go home, with no certainty that the request would be granted – in which case the request would depend on a level of trust that further rejection would not occur. Of the nine in the qualitative study who had become homeless after leaving home, six later returned home, and Joe, Janet, Polly, and Rosco were still living with their parents. Some may not want to return home, but in other cases, an invitation to return home may at least give them the choice. However, as with other forms of support (see Chapter 5), the initiative lies with the parent.

Leaving the door ajar

The ability to take the risk of leaving home may depend on a level of trust between a young person and their family that, should things go wrong, they can return home again. In such cases the door has, figuratively-speaking, been left ajar when they leave. Jean, Ron, Susan, Shona, Patricia, Kevin, Chris and Jai commented that they knew they could return home if it didn't work out, though further persuasion was required in Kevin's case, and Shona still needed an invitation from her mother. Many said that their parents would never reject them. Jai, for example, says his parents would never have shut him out, because they had been rejected by their own parents when young, and even Joe thought that his mother would not throw him out again. Some were specifically told by their parents when they left home they could always return 'if it doesn't work out'. It was comforting to know, for example, that one's room was still there. This kind of trust may extend, where necessary, to the wider family: Sandra and May both knew that, if necessary, someone in their extended family would take them in.

It may, however, be safest to negotiate one's return before leaving. An *if it doesn't work out* approach acknowledges the risk associated with leaving home, but at the same time indicates that failure may not be the fault of the leaver, but due to unforeseen circumstances. But it still does not come in a simple fashion, especially in Jai's case:

Mother said: 'If it doesn't work out you are going to have to come back'. And I was like 'Aye, I know. But if it does work out I'm not wanting you to give me a hard time because I'll have to stay'. And at the end of it, when I came back she was like 'Are you sure you want to come back?'.

Before she left home, Patricia asked her mother: 'If it doesn't work out can I come back?'. Her mother replied: 'Of course you can come back. Your room's there'. Later she had to swallow her pride and phone up to ask her mother to collect her, but her pre-emptive work had made this easier. In both cases, the way was open for a request to return home.

Without pre-emptive negotiations of this type, a young person may not ask to return home, for fear of rejection. Thus Sandra, who had been told to leave home did not want to risk a further rejection: 'We werenae going to come up to the hoose to get a deafie and no' getting in'. On the other hand, Axil (who can be characterized as a man of action rather than words) just took the risk and arrived back on the doorstep in a taxi; no questions were asked and no explanation given.

An invitation to return saves the loss of face associated with having to ask – and admit defeat. Power in these circumstances is clearly with the person making the invitation. Eric went home, he says, because they were always asking him to go back and there was nowhere else to go anyway. Similarly, Rosco went to live with his sister because she invited him: 'And I just leaped at the chance "Yes, yes, now!" I had a suitcase packed within minutes of her offering!'.

There are circumstances when returning home suits the interests of the parent at least as much as that of the young person. Chris's mother was lonely and asked him back, so he went. And as a child, Charlie was sent from his grandparents' to live with his father once he was old enough, because his father was lonely. His father's needs appear to have come first. May was needed at home when her father was ill, and cannot leave her mother now that he has died.

Closing the door

Some parents, and other family members too, seem to close the door behind the young person leaving home, and to take away the safety net. Eric's parents both told him to stay away at one stage. Sean has a history of being forced to leave, and doors closing behind him ('uprooted and nowhere to go'). He was told to leave home by his mother and step-father, and sent off to live with his father, whom he barely knew. He begged in vain to stay at his mother's, and he still hopes – years later – that one day he will be allowed to return there. Later his step-mother also refused to allow him to stay, though following mediation from his father, he was allowed to stay temporarily. His father was himself later turned out of the house. Charlie was sent to live with his grandparents when his parents split up, though his sisters remained with his mother; later he lived with his father, until the latter re-married and Charlie was given three weeks' notice by his step-mother, when she thought he had taken drugs. He did not wait the three weeks, but left on the spot. In these cases, the door seems to have been closed behind them.

There may still be scope for negotiation. In some cases, parents did not seem to mean it. Terry's parents said 'That's it, you're not coming back'; but she did (with a bit of persuasion) and her room was still there. Shona had a similar experience, when her father evicted her (though her parents were not united in this). Sandra's mother said 'don't bother coming back', but she was under the influence of her husband, who was later himself told not to return. Sandra returned home when her father eventually left it.

In a number of these cases, the young person has become embroiled in a broader problem of family relationships, and appears to become scapegoated for what is essentially a marital problem.

Unlocking the door

A problem may occur when asking for anything at a time when a young person is trying to prove that they are capable of independent living, since asking emphasizes the power imbalance between prospective receiver and giver, and risks rejection. Thus, it was the invitation from her mother that tipped the scales and decided Shona to return: 'It was great of her! I was half and half'. Asking to return may be seen as an admission of failure, but an invitation sometimes requires complex negotiation.

The invitation can be part of a game people play. Terry did not want to ask if she could go back, but it was a while before her parents took the initiative:

> I didn't want to ask to come home. I wanted them to ask me! 'Please tell me!' And eventually they said 'Look – I think you should, you know. I think you should come home'. And I went 'Aye, I'm about to. I'll go and get my bags now!'

Jill was in a similar situation, not wanting to ask: 'She was waiting for me to ask to come back and I was waiting for her to ask me to come back'.

The problem of negotiating an invitation may be so complex as to require a mediator. In two cases it was a sister. Joe's sister helped him get back home again by mediating with his mother. Jill manipulated her sister into mediating between her and her mother in order to engineer an invitation home:

> So I deliberately made a point of phoning my sister, and telling my sister that I had got all this stuff for my house, which was a heap of rubbish, but I knew fine she would run and tell my mum, and my mum would think 'Oh God, she's serious' [about setting up home].

In two other cases it was a parent. Ron's mother often mediated for him with his father: 'When I phoned and tellt her I was coming back, the old boy wasnae going tae let us in, but my mother persuaded him to let us back in'. Similarly, Sean's father mediated with his step-mother to arrange for Sean to go and stay there for a while, when he had nowhere else to live.

The invitation home may not be easy for the parent either, but may become easier when tied to a specific or changed situation. Thus, Joe's mother told him on his birthday that he could come home if he wanted to, while Sean's mother said 'Why don't you come down one Christmas?'. Sandra's mother invited her and her sister home when their alcoholic father left ('Do you want to just come back up the road now your dad's away?') – it had been because of his drinking that they had left home. Finally, Kenny's parents said he could go back home when he left the army ('They could have been a bit awkward about it. But they were fine'). As the survey findings indicated, returning home may present fewer problems when the reason for leaving home is no longer present, such as when a job or course ends.

Leaving home and cooling off

Leaving home because of rows with parents is common among earlier home-leavers, as the last chapter indicated, and the interview data above show how it can involve spur of the moment actions on both sides (parents throwing out or young person walking out). As we have seen, the problem is how to return later without either party losing face. Young's (1987:123) study suggests that leaving home because of conflict does not necessarily draw a negative response from the parents, who 'may accept the child's perception of conflict, and respect their need to live away from home for some time'. As Maas (1986:12) observes:

> Often it is necessary for some dramatic 'break' to occur so as to precipitate recognition on the part of the parents that their 'children' no longer exist and in their place are rapidly maturing young adults. Many instances of premature leaving are such periods of 'time out' and if changed relationships result there are rarely any repeated episodes until the young person finally departs in his/her own good time.

Relatives or foster parents may provide a temporary respite from family conflicts for young people, as some of our interviews showed, and cooling off periods away from parents may prevent more serious breakdown, though as Ainley (1991:94) points out, returning home after a cooling off period away can still be principally because there is nowhere else to go. Even so, it seems that in many cases it is the family of origin which, especially in the case of family conflict, has to make the first move if a young person is to return to the parental home. In this respect, the parents hold the key. Young's analysis (1987:127) of Australian patterns also supports this conclusion, suggesting that the reason for returning home which is most consistently associated with family conflict, and parents' disapproval of the original departure from home, is a return made at the parents' request.

Who cannot return home?

What happens when there is no safety net? Returning home is not always easy or possible, however much the government may wish to shift the burden of responsibility from the state onto the family. Young people who had left home but become unemployed were twice as likely to return to their parental homes if their fathers were in full-time employment, as when they were not (Jones 1991). The economic circumstances of the parental home are therefore likely to affect opportunities to return.

Comparison of the respondents to the Homeless Survey with respondents to the SYPS who had experienced homelessness showed that the former were less likely to have returned home to their parents. Respondents to the SYPS 1989/91 who had been homeless were probably traced in the postal survey precisely because they had maintained contact with their parental homes, and so they present a rather different picture of homelessness in some respects. Though they had left home for similar reasons to those in the Homeless Survey, they were less likely to have experienced family breakdown, or to have such large families, and their parents were more likely to be in full-time employment and to have helped them with money. They themselves appear to have had a better experience of education and the labour market, being more likely to have qualifications and be currently employed. Thirty-seven per cent of ex-homeless in the SYPS had returned home since leaving it, compared with only 12 per cent of respondents to the Homeless Survey.

We asked the respondents to the Homeless Survey (who were currently homeless, whether sleeping rough, or in a hostel, or staying in someone else's accommodation while trying to get a place of their own) whether they were thinking of returning to their family home to live, and if not, why not? (Figure 4.1). Only 10 per cent said they were thinking of going back home. Of the other 90 per cent, some gave practical reasons, such as that their parents could not afford to have them back (6 per cent), or because there was not room at home for them (13 per cent), or because there were no jobs in the area (4 per cent). For others, the problem continued to be their relationship with their parents: 4 per cent had lost contact with their parents, and 3 per cent specified that they could not ask, but by far the main reason for not returning (given by 43 per cent) was still because they did not get on with their families. In some cases this meant that they would be in danger of physical or sexual abuse if they returned home. Their ages ranged from 16–22 years, and the older ones tended to say it was too late, or they were too independent.

The 27 per cent of homeless respondents who gave 'other reasons' for

Figure 4.1 Reasons for not returning home, Homeless Survey

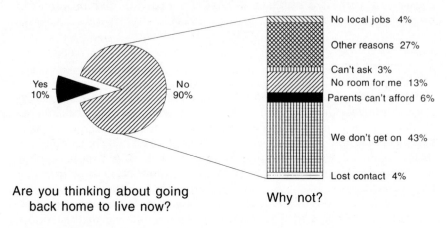

No local jobs 4%

Other reasons 27%

Can't ask 3%
No room for me 13%
Parents can't afford 6%

We don't get on 43%

Lost contact 4%

Yes
10%

No
90%

Are you thinking about going
back home to live now?

Why not?

Source: Homeless Survey 1992

not returning were asked to write them in. The list makes depressing reading. The main reason was that they liked their independence (n = 15), though some said more enigmatically that they 'did not want to go home'. Several said that their parents would not have them back, and in four cases there were court interdicts (injunctions) preventing them from returning home. Fear of abuse or violence was the reason given by eight people, and eight others said that they did not get on with someone at home. Issues to do with drink and drugs (which could be on either side) cropped up again. Another simply said there was 'nothing there'. In interview, many said that they would rather stay homeless than return home. Similarly, Stockley *et al.* (1993) report that some homeless young people they interviewed said they would only return home if their parent were dead.

One-third of homeless young people appear to have been in local authority care, as several studies have indicated. When they are discharged from care, there is usually no scope for them to return if independent living does not work out. Leaving care, as opposed to leaving home, is a one-way transition. This may be one reason why there is such a high proportion of care-leavers among the homeless.

Some homeless young people do, however, return to their parental homes. The parental home cannot necessarily be seen as a housing option, however. The question of whether a return home ends homelessness careers, or merely ends one episode of rooflessness, thus deferring the problem, is examined in Chapter 6. It is clear, though, that the current social security arrangements do not provide any kind of safety net to those who cannot turn to their families: very few young people are able to explain to social security staff why they are unable to return home, in such circumstances (see Peelo *et al.* 1990; Kirk *et al.* 1991), and without an income, they cannot stay in the housing market. The ability to return home is thus a crucial issue. Young people may choose not to return, but only some of them really have that choice.

Returning home can, however, be an important stage in the process of household formation, and it is important that this is recognized. More research on the significance of returning home is needed, especially since more young people, from a broader section of society, appear to be doing it. The relationships between young people and their parents are certain to be affected, but we do need to understand how. More thought also needs to be given to whether young people leaving long-term local authority care need a similar structure of support for when they leave care, and whether short-term 'respite care' should be provided for young people who are in conflict with their parents, to allow some breathing space on both sides.

For some young people, though, returning home is no longer relevant. They may have homes of their own – on their own, with partners, or with children – and foresee no further need of the parental home as a sanctuary or safety net. Support for setting up home is explored next.

Chapter 5

A supported transition?

It doesnae matter what age you are, ye still need somebody's help. Everybody will always need somebody, even just to talk to. I think that if you're gonna be independent it's wi' everybody's help. And you'll have to be independent at some stage of your life, I suppose, I suppose, but . . . you've got to be really grown up, you've got tae ken what you want to dae . . . You're no gonna tae have your mum there a' yer life to run back tae. (Zoe)

As they grow older, young people increasingly want to be able to assert their individual identities, and be both economically independent of their parents and emancipated from parental control. Parsons (1956:19) argues that it is one of the functions of families to help in emancipating the child from dependency. This family function currently receives little state support. Policies which extend young people's dependency make it more difficult for them to take their place in the adult word, and effectively undermine family life. A study by Hutson and Jenkins (1989) indicated that families absorb the additional responsibility of maintaining an unemployed young person, 'taking the strain', and thus present a coping front to the outside world. In this way, families may unintentionally collude with policy changes. In recent years, the strain on families has increased further.

Without access to the safety nets of unemployment benefit or Income Support (since the 1988 changes), and without a housing element in the allowance accompanying the training schemes which 'replaced' Income Support, it has become difficult for young people under 18 to set up home, even when they are able to obtain housing. Since deregulation of private sector rents in 1988, rents have increased, but Housing Benefit has not, for a variety of reasons, followed suit (see McLaverty and Kemp 1994), leaving many tenants worse off. With the withdrawal of the higher 'householder rate' of benefit in 1987 from those under 26, many lack the individual resources needed to sustain independent living. Even students have been affected, with the withdrawal of Housing Benefit and of their right to claim Income Support during vacations. Furthermore, state support for setting up home has been eroded or withdrawn: in particular, Exceptional Needs Payments (for furniture etc) to DSS claimants were abolished and replaced with loans from the Social Fund. It is difficult for those on social security or low incomes to save the deposit needed on a flat, when local authority Housing Benefit is paid in arrears. These changes have been part of a drive to reduce the cost of the welfare state and to 'privatize' its functions (Harris 1989; Jones and Wallace 1992). The effect has been a dramatic reduction in state support for the transition to adulthood. The availability of family support has become crucial.

Most of the state support for independent living was reduced as part of the policy to encourage young people to stay longer in their parental homes, or conversely not to provide an incentive for them to leave. Thus, the Parliamentary Under-Secretary of State for Social Security said in 1988, at the time young people's access to Income Support was being withdrawn or reduced: 'We recognize that there are circumstances in which people do have to move out, but we would not wish to create an incentive' (Hansard, 22 December 1988, col. 622, quoted in Kemp *et al.* 1994). The main remaining support for independent living comes in the form of Housing Benefit, received by 31 per cent of householders under the age of 25 according to Gibbs and Kemp (1993). A recent small-scale study by Kemp *et al.* (1994) found no evidence to suggest that the availability of Housing Benefit affected patterns of leaving home. It seems that without further and fuller evidence we can no more assume that Housing Benefit acts as an incentive to leave home, than that the non-householder rent deduction from parents' benefit acts as a disincentive to stay (c.f. Cusack and Roll 1985).

According to Walker (1988), the basic minimum cost of setting up home for two was around £1,200, while Kirk *et al.* (1991) suggest that a young person would need at least £1,500 for essential furniture and equipment, plus a weekly income of £43 (at 1990 prices) to set up and maintain a home. Many young people lack these resources.

This chapter will explore how and whether young people on 'component' incomes manage to make up the deficit and mobilize resources within their families in order to make the transition to independent homes. The question of what constitutes a viable income for young people leaving home is the subject of current research. Asking for help may be hard for young people who have already made some progress along the transition to economic independence from their families. Furthermore, it may be hard for people with families who are unable or unwilling to support them.

'Traditional family values'

The policy changes which have made family support more necessary have been cloaked in government rhetoric about 'traditional family values'. Marsland (1986:94), an academic with influence in Conservative Government circles, puts it thus:

> Young people need the support of their families and the family is seriously weakened as an institution if it loses its responsibility for young people. But genuine family responsibility for young people is make believe unless at least some of the costs of their care are shifted back from the state to the family.

Tradition is invoked as a justification for policy change based on an explicit intention to shift responsibility for young people from the state to the family. The policy is based on a static view of youth, as well as many false assumptions about family life.

Such policies mean that the state is increasingly seeking an active role in directing family relationships. Attempts to control, and enshrine in law, family relationships are not confined to the relationship between parents and their children. There have indeed been increasing attempts, as Finch and Mason (1993) indicate, to replace a complex moral framework of family obligations with a legal one. And therein lies a problem. These policies are based on assumptions about normative family practices. From their research on family responsibilities towards the elderly, Finch and Mason conclude that there are no fixed rules of family obligation ('the right to help must remain with the donor') and negotiation is therefore needed. The government may seek to increase family responsibility, but it cannot orchestrate the negotiations which must occur. Finch and Mason (1993:167) argue, for example, that:

> Claiming rights is definitely not seen as a legitimate part of family life. Even where one person accepts a responsibility to help, the other does not have the right to claim, or even to expect, assistance.

Young people, as we shall see, have similar difficulty claiming support from their parents. We have already noted in the last chapter how returns to the parental home were usually effected only after a parent had made the invitation; similarly, financial and practical help usually have to be offered rather than requested.

Government 'interference' in family matters can have unanticipated results. When forced by legislation to act in a way which is seen to be unfair, family members may resist. Finch (1989b:15) points out that:

> We know from past history that young people and their families *will* resist if official expectations about the financial relationship between them drift out of line with what most people regard as reasonable.

Finch points to the operation of the household means test in the 1930s as an example, where young people earning wages and living in the parental home were expected to support their unemployed parents; apparently, many took evasive action by leaving home, with the collusion of their parents (Crowther 1982; Deacon and Bradshaw 1983; quoted in Finch 1989a). It was in a similar vein that the Social Security Advisory Committee expressed concern that new Housing Benefit regulations forcing young people to pay their parents a contribution towards the rent might backfire, and that if the young people defaulted, the parent might 'force their "non-dependent" son or daughter to leave' (SSAC 1984), though there is no clear evidence that this has happened.

Family support and the transition to economic independence

Family financial help may perform an important function for young people leaving home, increasing their power in the housing market and helping to shape their housing decisions. Thus, Munro and Smith (1989) suggest that parental gifts are an important determinant of home-ownership, while Kennedy and Stokes (1982) have indicated the importance of family support with money to young Canadians facing high housing costs.

Not all young people receive financial support from their families, though. There are class differences, for example. Family financial help is particularly common in middle class families (Bell 1968). Several recent studies have indicated that as young people enter the labour market, financial support from their parents is gradually withdrawn (see Jamieson and Corr 1990; Jones 1992b). Even part-time working while still at school may result in a reduction in pocket money (MacLennan *et al.* 1985). Thus, while around two-thirds of 17-year-olds regularly received financial help from their parents over the previous year, by the age of 19, it was mainly students and children in middle-class families who continued to receive support (Jones 1992b). Wallace suggests that as young people become older, they are more likely to receive material support, such as food or clothing, rather than money. Research on young people in rural areas indicates that the economic relationship between young people and their parents is even less likely to be a financial one, and more likely to involve goods and services (Wallace 1991). This research would suggest that by the time young people are leaving home, they are no longer receiving regular financial help from their parents. Indeed, it seems that they are increasingly paying into the family budget rather than drawing on it, as they move towards a more reciprocal economic relationship with their parents (Jones 1992b).

In these circumstances, what happens when they need help to set up home? A study by Pickvance and Pickvance (1994a, 1994b) considered the mobilization of family help as a 'resource strategy' for young people entering the housing market, but found that only 7 per cent of their sample of 16–35-year-olds had received financial help specifically for their housing, though 28 per cent had received general financial help. The median amount of financial help received was £1,000. Where the help was for rent/mortgage or for housing repairs, the money tended to be seen as a gift, while loans were more likely for help with house purchase. Clearly, as the authors point out, parental help depends on their ability to help. It appears from the study that respondents tended to be somewhat over-optimistic about their parents' (and especially their in-laws') ability to contribute. There also remained a question of whether help had been desired or sought.

There may be many reasons, therefore, why financial help from parents may not be available. The remainder of this chapter examines first, issues of supply and need, and second, some of the problems associated with translating need into demand in the context of family relationships and the transition to independence.

Supply and need

Financial help from families depends in part (but only in part) on the families' ability to pay and the young person's need for help. This 'economic rationality' model (Cheal 1987) is over-simple, as we shall see, but it does indicate some general patterns. The SYPS allows an analysis of access to financial help from parents over the last year according to young people's current living circumstances, when respondents were on average $19^{1}/_{4}$ years of age. The latter provides some indication of need, since we can assume that though young people living at home will have living costs, nevertheless the living costs of those who have left home will be higher. Most of those who have left home and are still living away are students. Earlier research (Jones 1992b) showed that young people's own economic circumstances affected whether or not they received help: students, followed by teenage mothers, are most likely, young people in partnerships least likely.

Wealthier families in general provide more financial support than poorer ones. Young people living away from home (a picture dominated by students at this age) receive more help than those living at home. We can see from Figure 5.1 that there is some correspondence between supply and demand, since those who have left home and not returned are in general more likely to receive parental help with money than those living at home (this has also been noted by Pickvance and Pickvance, 1994a). Among young people who have left home, access to financial help from parents varies according to the financial circumstances of the family (Figure 5.1), thus 63 per cent of those whose father was in employment received regular financial help, compared with only 46 per cent of those whose fathers were not in employment. The family's economic circumstances thus not only affect provision of the family home as a safety net (we saw in the last chapter that unemployed young people were less likely to return home

Figure 5.1 Financial help from parents at 18 by father's employment status at 16 and leaving home status, SYPS

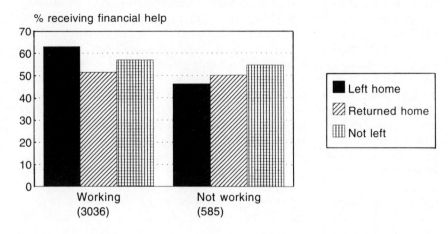

Source: SYPS 1987/89

Figure 5.2 Financial help from parents at age 18 by family structure at 16 and leaving home status, SYPS

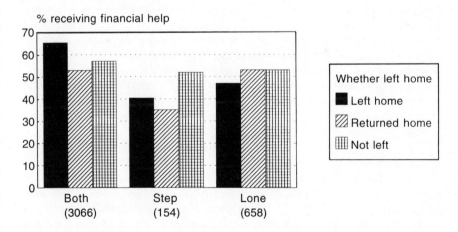

Source: SYPS 1987/89

when their fathers were also unemployed) but also affect family financial support. Family help out of the parental home is thus partly a question of supply and demand.

Survey data like these provide little evidence of family relationships, but Figure 5.2 indicates that financial support from parents is also affected by family composition. Here, there is little difference between those who have never left home. However among those who have left, it seems that those who lived with a step-parent when they were aged 16 were far less likely to be able to obtain financial help than those with both parents. Only 40 per cent of those with step-parents, compared with 47 per cent of those with lone parents and 65 per cent of those with both natural parents, received financial help. There is also a great difference between returners from step-families and those from families in which they lived with both natural parents. The indications are that step-children are less able to access family support when they need it. However, *need* is also affected by family structure, as Chapter 3 indicated: step-children tend to leave home before children in two-parent families, are more likely to leave home because of family conflict, and are more likely to become homeless. Step-children may thus not only have less access to family financial help but also have greater need for it than young people from two-parent families (in general). These survey data begin to suggest that family relationships are also an important factor, over and above the model of 'economic rationality'.

Negotiating family support

Family support is not a simple equation of need and demand, as Janet Finch and others have pointed out. At a micro-level within families, complex negotiation may be needed for family support to operate. Finch (1989b) describes the ambivalence inherent in the relationship between adult children and their parents and the difficulty in achieving 'the desired blend of dependence and independence'. The ways in which families negotiate issues of responsibility has been documented in research on unemployed young people's relationships with their parents (Allatt and Yeandle 1992; Hutson and Jenkins 1989) and earlier in a study of newly-weds (Leonard 1980).

   The remainder of this chapter is based on the SYPS follow-up interviews with people perceived to be at risk on leaving home. Available evidence, therefore, is based only on the young people's own accounts, and is centred on families which may have problems providing support because of unemployment or family breakdown. Research on what happens in other types of family, including intact families, families in employment, and middle-class families, is needed. The limited study described here (see also Jones 1995) nevertheless reveals both wide variation in access to family support despite some common elements of risk, and also many problems common to most respondents, which reflect their difficulties as young people trying both to become independent and to access support. Though the survey findings indicate that family breakdown tended adversely to affect access to parental support, the interviews reveal that support was even less likely to be forthcoming when a young person had been living with two natural parents, one of whom was incapacitated through illness or addiction. Further, the interviews revealed how family breakdown could have a variety of outcomes, including losing not only a parent but half the extended family, gaining a parent and new extended step-family, or the loss of both families.

Emotional support

The emotional climate of family life appears to affect the likelihood of family support, especially material and practical help with setting up home. Financial help does not coincide so greatly with family closeness (Jones 1995).

Emotional support is problematic, since it can also mean control (Leonard 1980), and closeness in families may prevent emancipation. This may serve a purpose for the parents but hinder the development of the child. Harris (1983:194) points to the opposition between the self-realization of parents and the autonomy of their children:

> The basic family 'situation' . . . becomes one in which the personal integrity of the parents can only be achieved by the sacrifice of the autonomy of the children, who are forced to reject their parents or remain forever emotionally dependent on them.

Parents thus need to be sensitive to the changing needs of young people as they grow older: too much protection can be as damaging as too little support, especially if this is accompanied by a withholding of autonomy.

Some families are more obviously emotionally supportive than others. Some say they can talk to their parents 'about anything'. Susan, for example, says that 'knowing that you had people to fall back on' has been important to her. But there was considerable variation between families. On the one hand were families such as that of Patricia, who at first presented a rosy picture:

> It's like *Bread* [a TV programme], it's like get round the table, 'What's the problem? What's their problem?' and it's sorted out within an hour maybe, and then we all go away and we're all happy again.

Later, Patricia complains of her parents' interference. At the other extreme are families like that of Janice, whose mother has never been supportive, ('I could never speak to her about anything', 'She just doesnae listen'), or Sean, who says: 'Emotionally, I never had anybody, not until recently. That's what all these grey hairs are. Twenty-two and I'm coming out in grey hairs.'

Reports of emotional support usually surrounded a critical event which had a major impact on family life. They included the death of a family member, the breakdown of a family relationship, and events such as pregnancy and leaving home. Zoe's parents were over-supportive when she had a baby, wanting to take over its care and not wanting her to leave home with the baby. The response of May's father to her pregnancy appears to have been at the opposite pole:

> His first words were to me – 'You can dae what the hell you like' he says 'but you're not marrying the bastard'. And he says to me 'How could you dae that to me? You of all people? I didn't think you'd ever do such a thing as that'. He stared at me for ages. It was horrible.

When she had a miscarriage at six months, her father said 'that was the way it was meant to be'; if the baby had been born, she would have had to leave home, because her father was 'no' having a brat running round my house'. Her father is now dead.

We tend perhaps to think that young people's conflicts are with both their parents, but we should not assume that when the relationship with one parent is poor, the relationship with the other parent is as well. Loss of contact with one parent should not inevitably mean loss of contact with the other. Family members and others may offer support by mediating, as the last chapter indicated, in the case of returns home. Mediation is a feature of family life, and family members may intervene in rows to keep the peace. Janice thinks mediation is important, 'Because I think at that age you even find it difficult to talk, to go places and arrange these things, and even to talk to adults'. Thus Eric's father mediated between him and his mother:

> He took me to the side and he says, 'Better start getting on wi' your mum', he says, 'Because I ken there's something going on between you and your mum' . . . He knew there was a tension there.

Some said that they preferred to 'sort things out' on their own. Whether this meant that help had been offered and rejected, or that the young person is justifying the lack of parental support, is not at all clear. We saw (in Chapter 3) how young people later defended their parent's action in evicting them, and this may be a similar phenomenon. Amy says she knows that her parents would support her, but: 'I like to try and sort out my own problems. I hate bothering people.' Rosco similarly says:

> I think I can manage on my own now. But they offer, you know. If they ever see something wrong, or if I'm down about something or if I need comfort or something, they would offer before I had to ask. Not that I would!

Later in this chapter this point will be taken up again. Rosco indicates the problem young people have about asking for any kind of help. This is a recurrent theme, echoed in talk about material and financial support, and, as we have seen in the previous chapter, in descriptions of returning home.

A changing parent–child relationship

Looking back over their teenage years, most felt they had now emerged from a difficult 'phase', during which they were having rows with their parents, rebelling against controls and unable to deal with their emotions. Some felt that their teenage problems were not of their making, and put them down to aspects of 'the system', or macro-economics or puberty, and that growing up was thus something which 'happened'; while others had a sense that their own actions had contributed to their maturing. Janet partially combines these two arguments: 'Your body's a' changing, obviously, and there's a lot of things happening wi' you, plus if you've got added worries of leaving home and that sort of thing'.

The transition to adult independence involves status passages, such as leaving home, starting a job, the formation of partnerships, the birth of a child. Each of these was experienced by those interviewed as a means of growing up as well as a status gain. Thus, the increased responsibility associated with forming a partnership and parenthood led to settling down, particularly among young men (see also Wallace 1987). Joe reflects on his difficulty in separating from his male peer group when he met his girlfriend:

> It's quite hard to get away from boy pals sometime. It's just – they're always trying to get ye – your best boy pals are always trying to get you back, know what I mean, if you're going oot wi' somebody.

Kevin also grew up as a result of meeting his girlfriend who already had a child. He is ambivalent about his new responsibilities and 'preferred it when I was young instead of noo. I feel auld noo. Wi' the wean and that.'

Leaving home is one of the major status passages through which transition to adulthood is achieved and most felt they had matured through it. In several cases relationships with parents improved as a result of leaving home. Peter says that before he went away his parents treated him like a child:

> They wouldnae listen to me. Everything you always done was always wrang. I was always arguing a lot wi' them. I still argue a lot wi' them noo, but it's mair positive arguments, it's mair constructive, it's no destructive this time.

He says that he grew up by being away from home, and his parents now recognize this:

> They missed a lot when I moved away. I grew up a hell of a lot. That's probably it. A whole lot aboot me they don't know. I'm probably a bit of an enigma, you know, they don't know how to take me. They've realized 'it's his life and he can dae what he wants to dae'.

Leaving home was thus clearly seen as a *means* of growing up, as well as a *consequence* of growing up. Zoe describes how her mother wanted her to stay at home, and how she felt the need to resist this: 'I had a lot of growing up tae dae'.

Several felt that their relationships with members of their families, mainly their parents, had changed as they themselves became more mature or 'mellowed'. Growing confidence may help young people handle relationships. Some felt they had reached a position in which they were on a more equal footing with their parents. This last is particularly important since transition to adulthood involves shifting power relationships as well as shifting economic relationships. Terry gets on well with her mother now: 'since I've sort of grown up more to her level'. Relationships with step-parents may also have improved. Joe gets on better with his mother's current boyfriend than with her last one, and thinks this is partly because he himself is older (and partly because the last one was 'a right creep'), and he also feels better able to talk to his mother. Sean says that it's only in the last few years that he has begun to get on with his mother, and cope with his step-father: 'My outlook on him has broadened a bit'.

These accounts suggest that as young people become adult, their relationships with their parents also change and may improve. Leaving home can lead to the improvement of a parent-child relationship, rather than represent confirmation of its deterioration. The willingness of parents to offer and their children to receive support may also change within this overall changing relationship. Regrettably, it is the younger people leaving home who are the most vulnerable and in need of support who are the most likely to have problems in their relationship with their parents and who have had their right to social security withdrawn.

Family support for setting up home

Burton *et al.* (1989) indicated that support for leaving home, including family support, was more likely to be forthcoming when the reason for leaving home was seen as legitimate. This is clearly a problem for those who left home as a result of family conflict. However, De Jong Gierveld *et al.* (1991) distinguish between family closeness (which may affect leaving patterns) and family economic resources (which may affect the success of the transition); thus their study indicated that young people leaving home for independence tended not to come from close families, but successful transition depended on economic support.

The case studies provided some support for these hypotheses. Family support varied according to the reasons given for leaving home.

- Four left home as part of a process of *family formation*, but only one returned home (Axil, when his partnership ended). The others were still living independently and had all received material and financial help from their families. Family formation normally represents a permanent move to independent living.

- Five left to take up a *job*, but all were now back at home, the move away having either been temporary or failed. Leaving home to take up work does not appear to be associated with a significant amount of family support. On the other hand, young people with independent incomes and moving into furnished accommodation may not need it.
- Leaving in order to gain *independence* does, perhaps surprisingly, attract family support. All four who left primarily for this reason had received emotional, material and financial support. However, two were currently back in their parents' home, Terry and Jai.
- Leaving because of *conflict with parents* is less associated with family support: five in this group of thirteen said that their families had been emotionally supportive, and only three reported that they had received material help, though around half said they had received financial help. Half were living in their parents' homes again. Those leaving because of family conflict may be the ones most in need of support for independent living and least likely to receive it.

Although all the young people interviewed had left home to live away at some stage before they were 19 years of age, more than half had returned home to live. Some of those living at home may have been hidden homeless, while others were taking an instrumental approach to living at home and using it as a means of saving. Five were saving up to buy homes of their own. As with all forms of family support, material and practical help must be offered on the basis of the young person's needs and the parent or other family member's resources.

The interview group can be divided into the following four sub-groups (Figure 5.3):

- *Supported returners:* those who received help in setting up home, but nevertheless returned to their parental homes.
- *Unsupported returners:* those who did not receive help, and returned home.
- *Supported independence:* those who are living away from home having received help.
- *Unsupported independence:* those who are living away from home, apparently without parental support.

Supported returners

In the first group are Jai, Terry and Janet. The first two are middle-class. Jai is trying to set up a hairdressing business and Terry (after her brief period of independent living in a furnished flat) is saving to buy a flat of her own. They both have instrumental reasons for living at home, and though paying board, appear to be making use of subsidized living arrangements. Just as leaving home can be a matter of convenience (as the reports of Shona and Rosco indicate in Chapter 3), so can returning home (see also Table 4.2). Janet returned home when her partnership broke

Figure 5.3 Parental help and householder status, SYPS case studies

Living in parental home

18[2] Terry		06[2] Joe	57[1,2] Patricia
69 Jai		17 Ron	67[2] Sandra
09 Janet		37[2] Polly	70 Chris
		46 Axil	75 Peter
		53 Rosco	92 May
			98 Kenny

Received help

Did not receive help

04 Eric	39[1] Shona	14[1] Janice	
13[1] Susan	42[1] Jill	60 Sean	
15[1] Jean	62[1] Kevin	81 Denise	
29 Amy	96[1] Zoe	99 Charlie	

Living away from home

Notes: 1 Living with partner
2 Saving to buy own home

down and there was a mix-up over her Housing Benefit. She had some help in setting up home, mainly with smaller things that her parents did not need any more; larger items, like a cooker and a suite, she bought second-hand herself. Now she has moved home again, she has brought her suite with her for her family to use.

Unsupported returners

No material help of any kind was reported by eleven people who were currently living in the parental home, though living at home is in itself an example of parental support (and not available to all). Some had moved into 'transitional housing' such as furnished rooms on leaving home; these include Ron, Polly, Axil, Rosco and Kenny. Transitional housing is more temporary and more associated with returns home. It also requires less support. The return home may only be temporary too: Chris and May both expect to move away again soon, May into a council tenancy as a lone parent. Some of those currently living at home were saving to buy somewhere more permanent to live; these include Joe, Polly, Patricia and Sandra. Shona (now in independent housing) had previously lived at home for this reason: 'If I hadn't been staying with my parents and trying to save up some money I wouldn't have been able to do it. I wouldn't have got something'.

Those who moved into furnished flats had little need of furniture or equipment, but others without family support and without fully-equipped flats had problems. Kenny had no such needs as he left home to join the army. Ron, Polly, Rosco, Patricia, and Sandra were currently in full-time jobs. Chris only had help from the DSS. Axil says his mother (a lone parent) could not afford to help, but expects help when next he needs it from the DSS (he is not aware that Exceptional Needs Payments have been replaced by hard-to-get loans from the Social Fund). Neither Joe nor Ron expects any family help in the future. Last time he left home, Joe managed to get second-hand things through his partner's relative, who had a warehouse. Ron says of his parents that if he left home: 'They wouldnae gie us nae help, like, but they wouldnae be worried aboot it'.

The people in this category appear to fall into three overlapping groups. There are those who are living at home and saving up towards independent housing, and who thus have instrumental reasons for remaining at home, even though they may prefer to leave. There are those living with a lone parent, who may be more able to help by providing a home than by providing financial support, as Figure 5.2 appears also to indicate; most of those with lone parents fall within this group of unsupported returners. And there are young working-class men, who as we have seen in Chapters 2 and 3 tend in any case not to leave the parental home until they establish a partnership one (Jones 1987a), and who like Axil (as reported in the previous chapter) may like the home comforts in the meantime. Some of these are also hidden homeless, though these are hard to identify – the criteria might include the quality of their relationships with their parents, and the amount of space afforded by the parental home, as well as their economic circumstances and housing preferences. For example, Joe, who lived with his mother but rarely communicated with her, or Patricia, who wanted to live with her partner but could not afford to set up home with him, might be regarded as hidden homeless. But the distinction between such cases and others where instrumental reasons for living at home might override other criteria of comfort, privacy and independence is very unclear.

Unsupported independence

Those without family support had to rely on their employers or the DSS to supplement their weekly wages or benefits, or resort to other strategies. Janice, Sean, Charlie and in practice Denise, had somehow managed to set up independent homes without family support. Janice, living with her partner, child and sister in a council flat, had a loan from her employer to get wallpaper and paint. Sean, who was also working, managed to buy some second-hand furniture cheaply at auctions, but is now in a furnished bedsitter. Charlie, on social security, lived on a camp bed for two months when he first moved into his council flat.

Denise gives a graphic account of what it is like to have to set up home on DSS help alone:

Ken what I mean, it's unreal – just no' fair. Because they dinnae help you at all. Turning roon' and telling me there's nae money in the Social Fund, I cannae get it. Oh, very nice! Thanks very much!

She managed by putting a little money by each week and 'like, a couple of friends gave us some stuff . . . which wasnae so bad'. Her story can be compared with that of Jill, on the next page:

Oh! I moved in here wi' a bed, that's what I had – a bed. I had nae carpets or nothing and like I claimed it a' off the Buroo [DSS], well I didnae get it a', I got a loan. I got that off the Buroo. I was getting £24 a week and I went up and I says to them 'Look, I've moved in, I need a cooker and that, I've got to eat'. They says 'You dinnae need a cooker tae eat, you're a single lassie – you dinnae need a cooker'. [They] says I dinnae need to eat, I could go and get stuff oot the chip shop and that! But how am I supposed to afford to get stuff oot the chip shop? 'I've got coal to buy and electricity to pay', I says, 'I've got poll tax to pay' – I didnae pay it, but you tell them that, ken what I mean, you've just got tae. I says, 'And buy food and a'? I've got tae dae a' that? And you're wanting me to come to the Job Centre twice a week as well as sign on, eh?'. I says, 'I'm going to be really slim, because I cannae afford the bus fare'. And he says, 'It doesnae matter, there's nae way you're getting emergency payment for a cooker'. I says 'And what aboot the rest of my hoose, what aboot carpets and that? I dinnae need a full suite, a chair will dae'. I never tellt him I had a bed. I got £200 to do the lot – carpet, cookers, wallpaper the lot. I dinnae ken why they even bother gieing ye that – it's no' worth it. And I went up and I fought wi' them aboot it and that, and that's what he says, that's all he would gie me. And they were wanting that back at £7 a week. I was like that – 'Oh aye, I'm really going to be rich here!' I was raging. I'd be starving by the second day in the week. Because that's what it was like.

Supported independence

Those who had received family help were mainly living in independent housing and not planning to return to their parental homes. They were nearly all living with partners (Kevin, Susan, Jean, Shona, Jill and Zoe). Susan (one of the few home-owners in the interview sample) and Zoe reported that their partners or their partners' families had also helped, while Kevin had moved into a flat which his partner had already furnished. Several in this group had children living with them: Jean, Shona, Jill, Kevin and Zoe. Several families helped with baby clothes, for example, as well as with help in setting up a home.

Susan's father rented her a flat which he owned, when she first left home. For the most part, support for setting up home was of modest proportions, provision of pots and pans, bedclothes, and other 'bits and pieces' which could now be spared from the family home. Much of this help was in 'getting started'; Jean and her partner had to rely on her family until they were able to save and get things second-hand for themselves. Amy (who moved into a furnished room) had help with 'bits and bobs' for leaving home, and her present bedsitter, at her aunt's house, is furnished. Jill's, Zoe's and Shona's families helped by buying large and expensive items, including carpets and cookers. Zoe, like Amy, would have preferred to do some of it on her own. Shona tried to obtain a loan from the DSS to get carpets and wallpaper, but 'they said I wouldn't get it because it's only things like bedding – they don't class wallpaper or carpets or anything like that as essential'.

Jill gives a description of the material, financial and practical support she had from her family (her mother, father and step-father) and friends in helping her during a series of transitions. First they subsidized her while she was pregnant and living with them, then they helped provide for the baby, then they banded together – virtually trying to outdo one another – to help her set up an independent home:

> Then when I got my house, I had picked up a lot of things myself, like I had been saving for years because I knew I would get a house. The only thing I was stuck with was the suite because it was the biggest and we had to lay out money to buy it. So my mum bought me the suite. My dad carpeted the whole house. Like my dad says he would match what my mum gave me. My mum gave me a £1,000 suite and my dad carpeted my whole house. And the kitchen when I came in was really, really grotty . . . I burst into tears when I seen it and I said there was no way – I was desperate for a house to get out my mum's house, but I kent there was no way I could have stood in that kitchen and cooked. It would have turned my stomach. So I burst into tears and says 'Oh God, I cannae cook in this kitchen. I cannae make baby's bottles with this gunge all over the place'. So my dad got me, paid for me to get a new kitchen. So they were really good to me. And like a lot of friends – I got a lot of stuff. And when my mother emptied a house, like my mum gave me a double bed and bought herself a new one. And I took my own stuff that had been in my own bedroom. So they both done a lot for me. And my step-dad – my dad's no good at decorating or anything – my step-dad decorated for me. So they all chipped in.

Material help for setting up home is not always exclusively given by parents, though parents were the most likely providers. Jill and Shona both indicated how several family members had 'chipped in'. In some cases, other family members, such as siblings or grandparents also assisted. People outside the immediate family may also have helped. Some had help from partners or their partner's families. Some also had help from friends.

Financial help

In contrast to material and practical help, financial support was less linked to setting up home. It was provided mainly by parents and consisted mainly of loans. When gifts were received, they were usually conditional or linked to something seen as worthwhile, such as help for a course (Terry, Amy and Jill), paying a deposit on a flat (Susan), rent or other debts (Susan, Jai, and Eric). Otherwise, gifts were linked to special occasions, such as birthdays or Christmas, apparently as a means of ensuring fairness of distribution between siblings (see also Allatt and Yeandle 1986, 1992). Resources may, however, not be equally distributed between children (Allatt and Yeandle 1992; Hutson and Jenkins 1987), and this was commented on by several of those interviewed.

Help more commonly came in the form of loans. Seven people reported unconditional loans from their families, and in three cases (Terry, Shona and Sean) the loan was related to the cost of buying or repairing a car (an essential in parts of Scotland). Some reported that they had financial help specifically to pay off debts. Thus Jai's father helped him pay a small rent debt once, and Susan's father helped when she had 'catalogue problems'. However, loans cause additional problems, since those most in need of help may be fearful of taking on yet another debt, albeit to their parents. Amy would never borrow anything 'mega big because I couldnae afford to pay it back'.

The need for help is not continuous, but may arise, for example if a young person becomes unemployed. Peter managed without parental help when working away from home, but has been paying a low rate of board money while unemployed and living at home. Similarly, levels of help depend on the family's economic resources. Though Eric says that the help he received from his parents 'was fine', nevertheless it was not enough because 'they couldnae afford to give me enough to keep a house and a wife and a kid'. In the Pickvances' study (1994a), it was noted that young people often over-estimated their parents' economic resources, but this does not appear to be the case here, at least with hindsight. Kenny says he would only have got more help if his family were richer 'but they give me all they can'. Axil says that his parents have enough worries with the mortgage. Joe, whose mother is a lone parent, says 'I think my mam's done a great job for the circumstances she was in. I think she's done brilliant.'

Support and control

Finding the right balance between dependence and independence, and thus constantly readjusting the level of support to take account of 'growing up' can be difficult. Too much support when a young person is trying to be independent can be experienced as unhelpful. It may indeed be seen as a form of control, as Leonard (1980) suggests. Patricia experienced support as interference: 'They've helped me more than enough and I didn't thank them for it. I didn't realize how nice they were at the time. I just thought they were interfering at the time.' Peter similarly says he would not want his family to help any more: 'Too many strings get tied then. You lose your independence. I've worked hard enough for it, to get it, and naebody's taking it aff me now, I'm afraid.'

There is an awareness that by giving financial help, a parent can buy an obligation. Zoe's case appears to be a good example of a mother's attempts to maintain dependence and closeness – and of her daughter's resistance. Her parents were reluctant to let go of her, and tried hard to keep her close. Zoe thinks that 'it's bad in a way [to get family support] because you're no' learning to get on wi' life on yer ain'. Her mother was constantly wanting to take over the care of her child, and Zoe left home in order to assert her own identity as mother. Even then, her mother was wanting to build an extension on the house for her, and when Zoe rejected this idea, to furnish her flat, but Zoe was determined to do it on her own. Zoe had to persevere to maintain her independence, despite continued attempts at subversion from her mother: 'And I got on alright myself, ken, and my ma was sending me money because I wouldnae answer the door or anything because I kent she was greeting' [upset].

Resisting dependency

We saw in the last chapter that while some young people enjoyed their 'home comforts', others resisted them by leaving home, or were anxious to insist how, though they had returned home, they were still independent (paying dig money, or doing the housework, for example). The significance of loans rather than gifts may be that the former may avoid a feeling of dependence. Terry describes how her parents have helped her, but is also anxious to stress her independence and emphasize that they have not spoiled her with gifts:

> I don't take a len of them, they don't give me money. They'll lend me money and they'll help me out any way they can, but they've no' got the money to splash out. I'm not spoiled or anything like that. I do everything for myself.

Asking for help with money becomes more difficult as a young person grows older, both because of the sense of renewed obligation it brings, and because it takes away the young person's sense of their own achievements. The message that young people found it difficult to ask their parents for help came across very strongly. Even where help is offered, there may be too many strings attached. McKee (1987) suggests that those receiving help may feel obliged to reciprocate, and the study reported here found that inability to reciprocate may make some young people unwilling to seek support.

To Amy, not asking for help is a matter of pride, but there are other factors. In the following extracts she refers to the feeling of obligation that would result, and the problem of incurring a debt. At one stage, she needed financial support to go on a course, but:

> I've got so much pride aboot asking people for money. I just wouldnae ask them, like my dad or my grandparents. But I knew I could have got it, but I wouldnae ask for it. Because I thought the longer I'm unemployed it would take me a year to pay it off and I just couldnae do it.

And at another stage in the interview she says of her parents:

> I mean, they offer me money, they offer to try and help me to get a job, to look for somewhere, but I'm so independent I want to do it all myself. I don't want anybody turning roond and saying 'Do you remember we got you this flat?' or 'Who got you this or that?' – casting it up to me.

Patricia and Denise would also prefer to deny that they need help. Faced with her parents' 'interference', Patricia pretended that she was coping:

> They always wanted to know what I was doing and if I had enough money. And I had like no money at all and I hadn't eaten for two days, and I'm saying 'Of course I've eaten, of course I'm getting on fine'. You know, I wouldn't say 'I'm really starving'.

Denise says that if her father did not help, she would be 'totally rookit', but does not like to ask him, because it feels like begging:

> See if I've nae money, absolutely really skint, I'll no go near him. It feels like begging even when you're going to your ain faither, ken. I dinnae like going and saying 'I've nae money, I need food, ken'.

Now that she is working, Denise is clearing her debts to her father. She wishes that DSS or bank loans were easier to come by, because she does not want to be indebted to her father and dreads borrowing money from loan sharks: 'But there's naebody I can turn roond to and say like "Can I hae a lend of this such and such money and I'll pay it back?" There's naebody I can say that to.'

So, asking for help follows a similar pattern to asking about returning home. In both cases the offer needs to come first, if only so that it can be refused. Some complex games are played during these negotiations. Chris maintains some discretionary power about whether or not to accept help from his father ('I don't expect anything of him or anything, but if he offers – well, if it's a good offer – I'll accept it, you know'). Rosco cannot ask for help from his mother:

> I won't ask and I'm just too much myself to ask somebody for any-thing like that, especially my ma, so she offers it and I refuse and then

she offers it again and I refuse. And this goes on for ages before I go 'OK, OK, I'll take it'.

This problem of initiating help, while applying to the majority, does not apply to everyone. Sean and Jai have both asked for help, though recognizing that this jeopardizes their independence. The anomaly is Axil, who though saying several times in interview that if you want help in life you should just ask for it ('if you don't ask you don't get'), in practice, doesn't.

Why should parents support their adult children?

Claims on parents for support may become more difficult as the boundary of responsibility between the state and the family shifts. Young people have varying opinions on the appropriate position of the boundary, and reveal a degree of confusion and disagreement about it. Jill stresses parental responsibility: 'I think if you have a kid you should be prepared to keep him, nae just till his sixteenth birthday, but till they ready to go on their own'. Terry, on the other hand, thinks that the present system is unfair, and that people who have left school should be able to claim social security, rather than be supported by their parents:

[Students] are out to better themselves, and their parents – why should they support them after they're 16? I mean, fair enough until you're 16, because you're at school and you're supposed to support your kids. But after 16, I think – even 18 when they leave school [then] – I think you should get something to yourself.

Several felt that the state should do more to help young people, rather than put all the responsibility onto parents. The current situation was seen as unfair both to young people and to their families. It jarred with those who could not see why their parents should support them, and who would prefer independent help from social security. It is important to note that young people see social security as a *means of acquiring independence*, rather than leading to a 'dependency culture' within a 'nanny state'. Independence tends to be thought of in relation to the family of origin in these accounts. To Jai, independence is:

Being able to stand on your own two feet, not having to rely on other people for money. I mean, I'm not totally independent ... I still go running to my mum and dad when I've had a quiet week at work or whatever.

He was not happy, therefore, when refused help by the DSS and told: 'Your parents will have to support you'. He comments on the vulnerability created by a situation in which his parents had the power to give or withhold support, so that if they hadn't wanted to support him, 'I would have been in trouble then. I'd have been in real trouble then.'

The problem of not getting help

Far from receiving financial support, some interviewees supported other family members. Sandra makes a major contribution to the family home, and helps her mother financially. Janice is the main source of family support to her younger sister, who left home recently and now lives with her.

What happens when young people do not get support from their families, at a time when state support may also be hard to obtain? Among the SYPS case studies, those without family support occasionally found help from other quarters. Charlie had considerable help from his one-time boss, who helped him get a council flat and encouraged him to resume contact with his mother. Janice managed to obtain a loan from her employer, which enabled her to decorate her flat. Others without employment were almost wholly dependent on DSS, or survived through petty crime or drug dealing.

Young people can thus enter a poverty trap, which in some cases can include homelessness. Nine of those interviewed became homeless for a while after leaving home. These were Eric, Joe, Janet, Janice, Polly, Rosco, Chris, Denise and Charlie. Of these, only Eric had family support when he left home. Family support thus appears to be an important element in the successful establishment of an independent home, and structural problems, including the inadequacy of young people's incomes and the lack of affordable housing for young people leaving home, are exacerbated when family support is not forthcoming. It is notable that only 32 per cent of young people (aged 16–22 years) in the Homeless Survey had received parental help with money in the last year, and of SYPS respondents who had become homeless since leaving home, only 44 per cent had received parental help with money, compared with 56 per cent of 19-year-olds nationally in the SYPS.

The consequence of the withdrawal of the state safety net and lack of access to a family one was, for many respondents to the Homeless Survey, no income at all. Some resorted to begging or thieving to survive, and many had high levels of debt. As a recent report by Strathclyde Poverty Alliance (1992) suggests: 'This exacerbates their accommodation situation and locks them into the most extreme forms of survival, succumbing to exploitation by drug dealers, money lenders and prostitution pimps'. But they have to survive somehow.

The function of family support

We have seen in this chapter how family support depends not only on a simple matching of ability to help and need for help, but also as far as we can tell on the quality of the parent-child relationship, the perceived legitimacy of demands for help, and on whether the young person can obtain help without taking a backward step on their transition to economic independence. Young people's ability to mobilize support from their families, therefore, varies considerably. Even where they can, successful departure from the family home may still require the additional help of a partner. Those living alone on social security without help from their families are likely to be living in extreme poverty.

Support for setting up home can affect a young person's location in the housing market, since it can be on a range of levels, from help with house purchase, to help with equipping a council flat, to offering a shelter which can prevent rooflessness. Accessing such support may, as we have seen, involve complex negotiation. The next chapter will consider some of the other strategies young people adopt to mobilize resources and improve their housing market situations, in the face of further structural constraints.

Chapter 6

The 'youth housing market'

However old they are when they leave home, young people need somewhere to live. This applies whether their leaving was envisaged as temporary or permanent, whether or not their families support them, and regardless of the reason they left. It is argued that policy changes over the last few years have made it more difficult for young people to find and afford housing which is appropriate to their needs as they embark on adult life. This chapter considers the range of housing lived in by young people leaving home and reflects on the inequalities among young people competing for housing. From a demand-side perspective, therefore, a 'youth housing market' is defined, most of which is on the margins of the core housing market. The reasons for the variation in housing demand among young people are explored, and 'housing consumer' types identified. The chapter develops further the notion of inequality and risk in the housing market, and considers the ways in which young people may take steps to reduce risk and increase their economic competitiveness. Finally, homelessness is explored. The concept of 'housing career' (Ineichen 1981) provides a theoretical framework, since it is important to maintain the idea that young people are living through a process of transition, and 'move-on' possibilities which reflect their changing economic and familial status are needed.

The demand side of the youth housing market thus contains a dynamic which reflects changing individual housing needs, as people gradually make a transition from the family home, to (perhaps) a single-person household and eventually into independent housing with a partner. This process of household formation is associated with movement in a housing career. Characteristically, the start point of a housing 'career' and its peak are similar in terms of housing type: the majority of housing careers begin and peak (by middle age) in home-ownership and council tenancies. Were it not for the reduction in the latter and the expansion of the former, brought about by government housing policies, there would be continuity between the generations, with children of working-class families living first as children and then as parents in council tenancies, while those from middle-class families would be likely to begin and end their housing lives as home-owners. This is partly because of varying patterns of inter-generational transfers, as seen in the last chapter. The picture has become more complex in the last two decades, as a result of the restructuring of the housing market. Additionally, there has been an expansion of the period of housing career between these two points (origin and destination), as more young people leave home to live in intermediate households in transitional housing statuses.

Defined cross-sectionally, in snapshot terms, the youth housing market can therefore hide other processes underlying the basic dynamic inherent in the concept of 'market'. It is my intention here to draw them out. Pickvance and Pickvance (1994a) similarly argue that housing affordability (the relation between housing costs and household income) needs to be understood dynamically. It is in part because young people move from one housing status to another that we can think of a continuum of risk in the housing market, with homelessness at one end. Unless otherwise stated, the findings reported in this chapter come from the SYPS 1987/89 cohort data and the Homeless Survey (Jones 1993b).

The 'youth housing market'

First, let us first consider the location of young people as a whole, vis-à-vis the housing market. Their location depends on a combination of supply-side and demand-side factors.

By the age of 19, over one-third of young people have left their parental homes, though 28 per cent of these have returned and are back in the parental home again, as previous chapters have shown. Some of the people represented in Figure 6.1 as living away from home may yet return to live with their parents; others will have left home for good. The types of housing in which they live reflect the permanence or impermanence of their current situations; some forms of housing are more insecure and temporary than others, and may be more associated with returning home or the risk of homelessness; others may be more secure and permanent, and more likely to be associated with a permanent move away from the parental home.

What kinds of housing do young people live in when they leave home? Where are they now in terms of the housing market, and their individual 'housing careers'? Most of those who have left home and are still living independently are not located securely within the housing market, but are on its margins, and at an early stage in their housing careers. In short, the youth housing market is as characterized by its insecurity as the adult

Figure 6.1 Housing at 19 years, SYPS

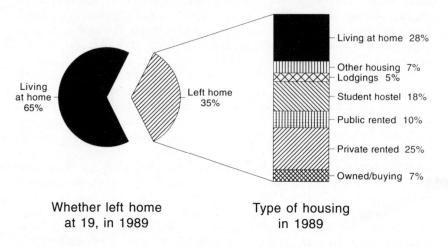

Living at home 28%

Other housing 7%
Lodgings 5%

Student hostel 18%

Public rented 10%

Private rented 25%

Owned/buying 7%

Living
at home
65%

Left home
35%

Whether left home
at 19, in 1989

Type of housing
in 1989

Source: SYPS 1987/89

housing market is by exclusion and inflexibility. At the age of 19 years (Figure 6.1), few were in public sector rented accommodation or in homes they were buying – housing types which we can think of as relatively secure 'destinations' in a housing career. Nor, indeed, were there many in accommodation rented from housing associations (though housing associations are increasingly housing young people, according to Williams, 1992). Instead they tended to be in 'transitional' housing which one might associate with a *youth housing market*.

The largest proportion were in rented accommodation in the private sector (and this sector is increasing: from 35 per cent of 19-year-olds who had left home in 1989 to 41 per cent in 1991, according to the SYPS), which tends to be more temporary and insecure, but may often provide the kind of flexibility in housing which young people at the start of their employment careers may need (Jones 1987a; Burton *et al.* 1988). It permits geographical mobility to a degree not afforded by local authority housing or home-ownership, and this can be important if young people are to take advantage of job and training opportunities. Furthermore, furnished accommodation, which forms a large part of this sector, cuts down the cost of setting up home for a young person embarking on independent living. On the other hand, the deregulation of the private rented sector is likely to have increased risk in this housing sector. A survey of private sector tenants found that over a quarter were suffering harassment and a third reported poor conditions or overcrowding (Sharp 1991). It seems that flexibility can only be bought at the price of security.

Others were living in other forms of 'transitional' housing, even further to the margins of the housing market. This includes students' halls of residence, nurses' homes, lodgings and job-related housing, such as in barracks or hotels. Accommodation such as this allows young people to leave home and take up low-paid and possibly insecure employment without having to compete in the housing market. A recent study of young people in rural Scotland indicated the importance of jobs which had housing attached, as a means by which young people could leave home, and the armed forces and merchant navy have traditionally fulfilled an important role in this respect, as more recently has hotel and catering work (Jones 1992a). This type of accommodation does not, however, provide security, since loss of job or student status will mean immediate loss of accommodation, in most cases. Nevertheless, without transitional housing, young people might be obliged to remain at home with their parents and accept the limitations of the local labour market, or to leave home with poor resources and face an even greater risk of homelessness.

Some had indeed been homeless. The SYPS 1989/91 indicated that 6 per cent of 19-year-olds who had ever left their parental homes had experienced homelessness since leaving home. Since most young people define homelessness in terms of the narrow media stereotypes of 'rooflessness' or sleeping rough, this is likely to be an underestimate of the incidence of homelessness in its broader aspects. In this chapter, homelessness is defined according to the broader UN definition which includes emergency accommodation, such as hostels, and insecure accommodation, such as temporary accommodation in other people's homes, or 'hidden homelessness'. Official and other definitions of homeless are discussed by Johnson *et al.* (1991). Greve (1991) points to the unwillingness of central and local government to accept the broader definitions of homelessness, an unwillingness which, he suggests, is explained by the magnitude of the task and the resources which would be involved in tackling it.

Greve (1991) suggests that the overriding cause of homelessness is the critical and growing shortage of affordable rented housing. Policy changes in the last decade or so have affected both the range and amount of housing available to young people, and their ability to afford it. We have seen how the volume of demand for housing has nevertheless increased. Expectations have also been raised. As a result of the increase in home-ownership in Britain, there is a greater expectation among young people that they will become home-owners rather than council tenants. However, young people leaving home are unlikely to be able to take on a mortgage. The alternative, council housing, has never really catered for the needs of young single people and is even less likely to be able to do so now that the focus has moved onto social housing. The cheap, and usually furnished, end of the private rented sector is therefore still the main sector entered by young people leaving home, but though there appears to have been an increase in take-up within this sector (Jones 1993b), recent research suggests that deregulation has mainly benefited higher status tenants (Rhodes 1993), instead of increasing the quality throughout. Overall, it seems that to compete in the housing market, young people have to have a high level of financial resources. The alternative is to belong to one of the social groups which qualifies for social housing.

To some extent, therefore, the structure of the housing market will structure demand-side inequalities, forcing a polarization between those who can pay for home-ownership and those who can apply for social housing. The problems are: first, that the demand side of the youth housing market seems to form a continuum between these two extremes, and thus does not fit housing provision; and second, that the structure of life course transitions involves movement within the housing market, which lacks the flexibility to cater for this.

Inequalities in the housing market

Alongside these changes in the policies affecting housing supply, and themselves structuring demand, there have also been policy changes affecting young people's economic competitiveness in the housing market. Affordability in housing supply is not only a question of putting a supply of appropriate housing into the market place. Young people are a heterogeneous group and have differential ability to compete in a market which is restricted and therefore geared to competition. Though young people as a whole face problems in the housing market, inequalities between young people result in some having more problems than others.

Different forms of housing are occupied by people in different circumstances, reflected in their stage in the life course and their social grouping. In order to understand the sources of this housing variation, it is important to understand the sources of variation on the demand side – i.e. between young people – on these two dimensions, the one longitudinal and concerning process, the other cross-sectional and concerning the social structure. Only thus can we understand both housing demand in youth and the structures which affect young people's chances in the housing market, increasing opportunities for some and increasing risk for others. Let us think first how this operates in theory, before looking at empirical evidence.

Figure 6.2 puts the factors affecting inequalities in the housing market into a conceptual model, showing the relationship between them. The model suggests that housing demand varies principally according to the type of household seeking housing, although there is a return effect, and housing supply is likely to affect household type, as we shall see. Household type is itself partly determined by the stage in a young person's transition to adult life; this can be seen as a multiple transition along various interconnecting paths (into the labour market, into family and household formation, as well as into the housing market) and is reflected in their current economic, marital and parental status. Stage along any of these paths may be partly determined by age, but only partly, since patterns of transition vary according to social class and gender (Jones 1988).

Figure 6.2 Structures of inequality in the youth housing market

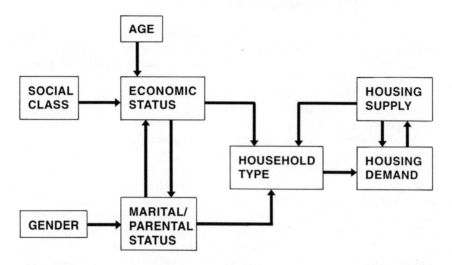

Inequalities resulting from social class and gender continue to affect transition to adulthood, including patterns of leaving home (Jones 1987b; Jones and Wallace 1992; Bates and Riseborough 1993). Working-class transitions tend to be more condensed and to start earlier, while those of the middle class tend to be more protracted and to start later (Jones 1988). Thus, it is more common for young people from working-class families (in which fathers are in manual work) to become economically independent of their families of origin earlier than young people from middle-class homes (in which fathers are in non-manual work). Young women tend to form partnerships and start families earlier than young men, there being on average a two-year age difference between husbands and wives, though the difference in age is smaller when both partners have been in post-school education. Transitions in youth are further structured by legislation affecting access to an independent income, as discussed in Chapter 1 (and see Jones and Wallace 1992).

Housing demands will vary in their volume and nature according to household structures, but these will also vary according to the types of housing available. Thus, for example, a young person might seek housing alone, if appropriate housing exists, or may join forces with friends, if this gives them more power and choice in the housing market. This can be regarded as a form of 'housing strategy' (Pickvance and Pickvance 1994a, 1994b), a means of optimizing one's chances in the housing market and also of decreasing risk. The Pickvances (1994b:15) argue for a dynamic model of housing and household behaviour that:

> In contrast to the usual approach to housing behaviour which sees it as undertaken by a pre-existing household with a given income, we

see the formation of households and the resources they acquire as in part a response to housing conditions.

Strategies are not always possible. For example, the emphasis on providing emergency accommodation for single homeless or the new foyer initiatives (Joseph Rowntree Foundation 1991; Crook and Dalgleish 1994) providing hostel accommodation for single workers may make it more difficult for many young people to develop and maintain relationships with partners, in the 'normal' process of transition to adulthood. They remain single-person households.

Housing constraints thus affect household structures, supply modifying demand, as well as responding to it. In some situations, household strategies can be employed. These may be conscious or unconscious, and can cover a range of possibilities, from ways of avoiding homelessness to ways of climbing up another rung on the housing ladder. They may take the form of delayed home-leaving, returning to the parental home or living with other kin; getting a live-in job; boarding in a private flat or house; sharing accommodation and expenses with peers rather than becoming sole householder. Buying a home may be considered a housing strategy when rented homes are scarce, but for young people this strategy is not always available. Another strategy, perhaps more appropriate to young people who are undergoing so many life course transitions, might be use of the range of 'transitional housing' forms which may be more flexible and appropriate to young people's overall needs. Further strategies have been identified, including women cohabiting in order to have accommodation (a practice noted by Hutson and Liddiard, 1991), or, according to one prevailing myth, becoming pregnant in order to be housed in council rented accommodation (a hypothetical practice unevidenced by research but the subject of a common myth – see Clarke, 1989, or Greve, 1991, on the myth itself).

The concept of home, as we have seen, combines notions of household and housing. It is not surprising, therefore, that household career and housing situation are so closely linked.

Household careers

Household formation has often been an extended process, as Chapter 2 indicated. A conceptual model of household careers is shown in Figure 6.3. Four types of household are defined: parental households, intermediate households, peer or single independent households, and partnership households (Jones 1987a, 1990; Jones and Wallace 1992). People tend to move from the *parental home* into independent households, often via an intermediate household stage. *Intermediate households* are ones in which the young person may be living in what could be considered a 'surrogate

Figure 6.3 Household transitions

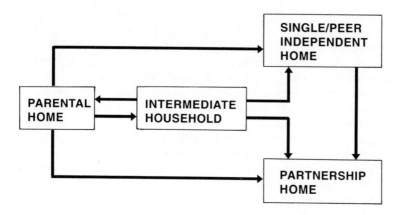

parental home', for example with relatives, or in group housing such as a barracks or nurses home, in which neither they nor their peers are the heads of household. The *independent households* may be partnership homes, but it appears that young people increasingly set up home alone or with their peers, sometimes as a precursor to partnership living (and thus part of the extended current process of transition to adulthood), and in these household types (single independent and peer independent households), young people appear to be far more emancipated from parental authority than those in intermediate households. The movement is not necessarily one way through this process, however. People often return to their parents' homes after having left. Intermediate households are likely to be the least permanent and secure types of household, and this is reflected in the types of housing lived in; in consequence, it seems to be mainly from intermediate households that people return to their parental homes.

It is important to maintain the notion of process when thinking of young people's current circumstances, though it is questionable whether either the housing market, or arrangements for housing young people who are homeless, allow for this. Paralleling household and housing transitions are education-to-labour-market transitions and family formation ones. Location along one transition path affects location along another. Thus, a young person's stage in their education and employment careers (as measured by their current economic status) and their stage in their family formation career (as measured by their current marital and parental status) both affect the type of household in which they live. They also affect their market competitiveness and the nature of their housing need. It is out of this combination of factors that young people in different circumstances become different types of 'consumer' in the housing market, and, in interaction with housing supply constraints, consumer 'strategies' may emerge.

Housing careers

Stage in the life course (as reflected by economic and family status as much as by age) is therefore an important variable when considering housing need. Housing demand in youth can be defined in terms of 'housing consumer' groups: single people in the labour market (whether or not they are in employment), single people in education, young couples and lone parents (Jones 1993b), which reflect stage in transitions relating to education, employment and family formation. Each housing consumer group is in a different position in the housing market.

If we look at the housing market location of young people according to their household careers and their current economic and family status (which interact to create different 'housing consumer' groups), we can see the full extent of heterogeneity in the youth housing market. Table 6.1, supplemented with other findings, forms the basis of the following discussion (see also Jones 1993b).

Intermediate households

For many young people, the first step into the housing market occurs when they move into an intermediate household. This was seen in Chapter 2 to be a continuation of a long-standing tradition among young people leaving the parental home for reasons other than marriage. Intermediate households are therefore relatively less common among older working-class males, who were seen to be the most likely to leave home to marry and thus move directly from the parental home to the marital one. Intermediate households include a range of circumstances in which young people may be living in other people's households: those of friends, relatives etc., or in surrogate households such as hostels or barracks. As Table 6.1 shows, they are found mainly in lodgings (27 per cent) and are well represented in 'other' types of housing (which include job-related housing). Like peer households, intermediate households are largely associated with full-time education or full-time paid work. Amongst paid workers in intermediate households, 31 per cent were in 'other' accommodation, associated mainly with their jobs, and 22 per cent were in lodgings. Other sectors are also well represented here, since some of these households are headed by a relative of the respondent. It is among students in this sector that we find the highest proportion in lodgings (37 per cent).

Job-related housing represents an important means of leaving home for young people with few resources, and entry into the armed forces has traditionally been a means of making the transition out of the parental home for young men in the rural areas of Scotland. Similarly, nursing, catering and hotel work can offer accommodation as well as a job for many school-leavers, just as student halls of residence can provide for those in higher education.

Intermediate households, therefore, appear to fall into two main types:

Table 6.1 Tenure and household type at 19 years by sex, SYPS

MEN	Type of household					
Tenure type	*Parent* %	*Partner* %	*Single* %	*Peer* %	*Inter.* %	*All* %
Owned	61	32	15	5	6	48
Council rented	32	39	17	4	15	27
Housing assoc. rented	3	2	4	4	3	3
Rented privately	2	10	9	42	25	8
Lodgings	1	7	8	5	26	3
Students/nurses residence	0	0	29	28	6	6
Other hostel	0	0	2	1	0	0
Other housing type	2	10	15	11	20	5
Row %	76	2	6	13	3	100
All (= 100%)	(1,528)	(41)	(117)	(257)	(69)	(2,012)

WOMEN	Type of household					
Tenure type	*Parent* %	*Partner* %	*Single* %	*Peer* %	*Inter.* %	*All* %
Owned	61	29	9	7	10	45
Council rented	33	34	35	3	7	28
Housing assoc. rented	3	4	7	3	4	3
Rented privately	1	20	16	48	12	11
Lodgings	1	1	2	5	27	2
Students/nurses residence	1	0	25	30	18	7
Other hostel	0	0	1	1	6	1
Other housing type	1	11	5	4	15	3
Row %	67	8	6	15	4	100
All (= 100%)	(1,578)	(178)	(139)	(350)	(98)	(2,343)

Source: SYPS 1987/89

institutions such as barracks, student accommodation, or hostels; and households in which the respondent is living as a lodger perhaps, in someone else's home. In the former circumstances, the accommodation may be job or course-related, and so the security of the accommodation is tied to that of the course or job; in the latter situation we might expect to find 'hidden homelessness'.

Peer independent households

Peer independent households are mainly associated with the (growing) student population, rather than other groups: 36 per cent of men and 44 per cent of women in higher education were living in households of this type (compared with a maximum of 6 per cent among those outside the full-time education system). Further education students are less likely to have left the parental home. Inequalities between university students can however emerge: a recent study of student housing in Edinburgh (Nicholson and Wasoff 1989) contrasts the many students who were renting rooms or flats in the private sector, with the few who were able, usually with the help of their parents, to buy flats and become landlords themselves, renting out rooms to less advantaged students.

At a time when housing has become more expensive and less affordable for most young people individually, some young people pool their resources and share accommodation with their peers. This too can be regarded as a household strategy (Pickvance and Pickvance 1994a) which can optimize chances in the housing market by reducing housing costs and increasing household incomes. Peer independent households (see Table 6.1) are predominantly in the private rented sector (42 per cent of men and 48 per cent of women), or in students' or nurses' accommodation (29 per cent overall). Other tenures are barely represented. There are no great gender differences within this category. Typically, the category is likely to include students living together in a shared flat. In all, 49 per cent of students in peer housing were living in private rented accommodation, and 33 per cent in students' or nurses' accommodation.

Though the largest proportion in peer independent homes are students, and peer independent housing may be increasing purely as a result of larger student numbers, there may also be a new phenomenon of young workers sharing accommodation. Shared flats are mainly in the private rented sector (34 per cent) (Jones 1993b), but some local authorities are now housing young people in shared flats (Glasgow District Council's 'scatter flats' are an example). Shared flats have their problems as well as their advantages. They are not always popular, either because of the difficulties of sharing (Chapter 4 showed that some young people return to their parental homes because they could not get on with their flatmates) or because of the location of much of the accommodation.

Single independent households

Single independent households are becoming significantly more common among young people, as Chapter 2 indicated. Here, they include young people living alone or as lone parents with their child. Overall, 27 per cent are in council rented accommodation, and 12 per cent in owned housing, but Table 6.1 shows that it is mainly women who are in council rented accommodation (35 per cent, compared with only 17 per cent of men). Men are more likely than women to be in lodgings (8 per cent of men and 2 per cent of women) but less likely to be in private rented accommodation (9 per cent of men and 16 per cent of women). However, the category also includes those living in nurses' or students' accommodation (29 per cent of men and 25 per cent of women) and overall 11 per cent living in another type of accommodation, so it appears that there is a problem of definition and some people describing themselves as living alone may in fact have their own rooms in hostel accommodation.

Again, home ownership is associated with full-time paid work (with 19 per cent of those in paid work living in owned housing), but there is wide variation in the housing situations of those in employment: all tenures are well represented, except lodgings (only 5 per cent). Those in full-time education, on the other hand, are mainly in students' or nurses' accommodation (61 per cent), and are also well represented in the private rented sector (16 per cent). Lone parents are predominantly in the public rented sector (94 per cent), as are those who are unemployed (63 per cent).

Partnership homes

Young women are generally less likely than men of the same age to be living with their parents, and more likely to be living with their partners. One-third of all women were living away from the parental home, compared with only one-quarter of all men. Since women tend to enter partnerships and start families younger than men, it is mainly women who at 19 are living in partnership homes. Only 2 per cent of men at 19 years, compared with 8 per cent of women, were living in a partnership home (Table 6.1). The male partners of 19-year-old women are likely to be older and thus have more secure jobs and higher incomes. Some young couples, however, live with parents or in-laws, or in accommodation which they share with others. According to the SYPS, 13 per cent of young people in couples were living with their parents (and the figure would be somewhat higher if in-laws were included). Rauta (1986) indicates that this is most common among young working-class couples. Partnership homes are defined here as homes in which partners live without other peers and without their parents.

The types of housing lived in by couples tend to be more firmly situated in the housing market. Typically, in the recent past, council housing was an option for young couples with children, while home-ownership was an option for dual-earning, childless ones who were prepared to defer family formation (Murphy and Sullivan 1983). The polarization of the housing market thus re-enforced social class inequalities, and inhibited movement from one sector into the other (Ineichen 1981), at least until home-ownership was promoted through state subsidies in the 1980s. Home-ownership is, however, associated with older couples, and not only childless middle-class ones. Seventy-two per cent of couples (in which one partner was aged 19 years) were living in partnership homes, according to the SYPS 1989. Most young couples are living in public sector rented accommodation: 39 per cent of men and 34 per cent of women are in housing rented from the council. Seventy-eight per cent of housewives with children live in public sector rented accommodation, rather than homes which they own, as do the largest proportion (50 per cent) of those who are unemployed (Jones 1993b). The option of council housing is, however, decreasing among couples since the emphasis on social housing results in targeted groups getting housed ahead of those on the waiting list.

Home-ownership, on the other hand, is likely to be associated with childless couples. Thirty-two per cent of men and 29 per cent of women with partners are living in accommodation which they own or are buying. Home-ownership is mainly associated with those in paid work (41 per cent), though a few in full-time education or unemployed are also living in homes which they and/or their partners own. These are very high proportions given the age group. Ownership at this age and stage in the life course could be more of a liability than an asset during a recession which is affecting job security, mortgage interest rates and house prices, and which has resulted in stagnation of the housing market. Both Wallace (1987) and Mansfield and Collard (1988) suggested that newly-weds setting up home tended by preference to buy a house or flat if they could. Government policies made home-ownership the most economically rational course (until the recent property recession, that is) for those who could afford to take advantage of the subsidies offered (Crow 1989a). Perceptions of home-ownership may since have changed, though. It has become more difficult for young unmarried couples to buy since 1988, when dual tax relief was abolished. Since the recent housing slump, mainly in the south-east of England, some may find home-ownership less attractive and more associated with risk than in the previous decade. A recent study found that first-time buyers were among those most likely to suffer 'negative equity', their mortgage debt exceeding the fallen market value of the property (Forrest and Kennett 1994).

Risks and strategies

Each of these 'housing consumer' groups may face housing problems and some people face the ultimate risk of homelessness. It is useful to maintain the idea of housing demand as along a continuum, even though housing supply may be polarized. Risk is increased partly because of this lack of fit. The concept of housing career should not be so rigidly constructed as an upward movement as to deny the possibility that it can, as with employment careers, involve losses of status as well as gains. Coping strategies may come into play as a means of alleviating risk, even among those at the higher levels of the housing market. Forrest and Murie (1994) note that 'trading down' in home-ownership has been a response among some buyers to the risks associated with the recent property recession.

Young workers leaving home, often on low incomes, and if they are under 18 with no safety net of state support if they lose their jobs, may find it particularly hard to find appropriate housing either alone or in shared accommodation. This may be why relatively few leave home unless they can get housing through their employment. The other groups have problems too: the economic recession and the decline in public sector housing will make it more difficult for young couples or lone parents to leave home and set up independent households. The housing recession, changes in tax relief, and high levels of unemployment have made home-ownership a less attractive prospect for many young couples. The reduction in public sector housing supply and its increased targeting means that the traditional and safer alternative to home-ownership involves long waiting lists and the possibility of being re-housed in a hard-to-let flat in a deprived neighbourhood. Students, now deprived of income support and housing benefit, will not be able to compete in the deregulated private rented sector unless they can get financial help from their parents, and as has been suggested recently, may become more likely to stay at home. The financial difficulties many students now face may result in an increase in dropping out rates from colleges, and more students may find themselves living in insecure and overcrowded accommodation.

Chapter 4 noted that young people would often return to their parental homes if their partnerships, courses or jobs ended. However, the findings also drew attention to the fact that many young people could not return to their family homes. Loss of a job, dropping out of a course or the break up of a partnership can all be associated with loss of housing and financial problems. The conceptual model shown in Figure 6.2 was originally intended to describe the ways in which housing demand was structured in youth. It also, it seems, can be used to show how risk is structured.

Greve (1991) indicated that the problem for young people trying to enter the housing market was a lack of affordable accommodation. We have seen the diversity in types of accommodation entered by young people, according to their 'consumer group' (their economic and household status). As individuals, young people lack the resources to be competitive in the housing market; as couples or in groups they may enhance their housing chances and increase choice. This is where strategies come into play, as means of supplementing 'component incomes' to allow independent living. In the last chapter we saw the role of family support. Here we consider other means of enhancing housing market position.

Coping strategies come into play when real freedom to choose in the housing market is limited or non-existent. Pickvance and Pickvance (1994a) propose a strategic model of housing behaviour which goes beyond the idea that supply constraints affect housing preferences to suggest that household composition, income and expenditure are also a response to housing conditions. Thus, they argue, individuals take decisions on what household arrangements to make (e.g. whom to live with, when to have a child), what income to seek and what expenditure patterns to adopt (e.g. the balance between housing and non-housing items), partly as a response to housing constraints.

Strategies such as these may help young people get onto or up the

Table 6.2 Median housing costs by tenure and household at 19 years, SYPS (among those reporting housing costs).

	Type of household				
Tenure type	Parental £	Partner- ship £	Single indep. £	Peer indep. £	Inter- mediate £
Owned	15	50	35	40	20
Council rented	15	20	8	20	20
Housing assoc. rented	15	20	4	25	19
Rented privately	15	38	30	27	30
Lodgings	20	8	21	25	30
Students/nurses residence	–	–	25	25	22
Other hostel	–	–	19	25	21
Other housing type	15	23	7	18	15

Notes: 1 Table only contains groups where n > 10.
2 There is considerable variation in some of these categories – especially single in council accommodation, and partnership owned.
Source: SYPS 1989A

housing ladder, or may just prevent them from being recognized as hidden or potential homeless (Greve 1991). The strategies may simply defer the problem, rather than solve it, as Burton *et al.* (1989) have suggested. Rauta's (1986) study of young unmarried people living with their parents suggested they did so from choice, because there was someone else to take responsibility for domestic tasks, because it was cheaper and because of the company and atmosphere of the parental home; and as we have seen, other young people can sometimes benefit from living with their own parents, by saving on their housing costs and putting the money towards setting up home. The issue of concealed homelessness is therefore a problematic one.

A brief examination of the housing costs of young Scots (Table 6.2) shows the variation in median housing costs according to housing tenure and household type, at 19 years, in 1989. Living in the parental home appears to be a relatively 'cheap' option, in comparative terms, since the median housing costs of those living with their parents were £15 per week (see Jones, 1991, for a fuller account of 'dig money' practices). The most expensive housing tenure option was buying a flat, and partners who were home-owners paid £50 per week median rate for their mortgage, while single home-owners paid £35 per week. Council and housing association rented accommodation cost a median of £20 a week to this age group, representing a cheap housing option. The cost of public sector housing appears to be even cheaper in the case of many single independent households (which include lone mothers with children). The private rented sector, at a median £27 for peer households, £30 for single households, and £38 for partnership homes, was the second most expensive form of tenure. Within this sector, it is therefore cheaper to share with friends than to live alone. Students' and nurses' accommodation, at around £25 per week, was only slightly cheaper. Hostels and lodgings, both very insecure forms of tenure, do appear to be a cheaper 'option' than the private rented sector, for those who are unable to obtain more secure or higher standard housing.

So, living at home is certainly cheaper than living away from home for most people, but there are exceptions. First, it would seem that there are some circumstances where young people in council or housing association rented accommodation are paying less than those living with their parents; this group is likely to be young parents who are receiving help with their housing costs from the DSS. Secondly, single people living in other types of accommodation are paying less for their housing costs. As stated previously, many of these other types of accommodation are job-related, and may represent subsidized housing, but the category would also include institutions such as prison or hospital. In general terms, then, living with parents, living in job-related accommodation, and living in public sector accommodation with help from the DSS, all represent forms of subsidized housing (subsidized by parents, employers or the state) used by young people.

'Strategies' for entering the housing market may therefore include household strategies or resource strategies, such as:

- living in the parental home or with relatives
- pooling resources by sharing with peers or living with a partner
- getting a job with accommodation attached
- qualifying for subsidized social housing.

Where strategies have failed?

Not all young people are able to gain a secure foothold on the housing ladder, perhaps because they cannot compete for the limited housing which is available. The weaker the position a young person is in, the more likely are any strategies they use to be survival strategies, to see them through an immediate crisis, rather than strategies involving longer-term goals. Recent research, based on a sample drawn from hostels, day centres and soup runs, has indicated that the vast majority of homeless people of all ages are men (Department of the Environment 1993), but among young people aged 16–25 women outnumbered men in hostels (Anderson 1993), while men outnumbered women among those sleeping rough (Smith and Gilford, 1991). Women are also believed to be over-represented among the 'hidden homeless', living in situations where their homelessness is less visible.

The survey of homeless young Scots produced a sample of 246 young people aged 16–22 who appear to have failed to avoid homelessness. Most had slept rough, or been 'roofless' at some point, and sometimes for long periods of time: 21 per cent for over a month. Women were less likely to have slept rough than men, and it seems that this may be because of the personal dangers involved, since women were far more likely to have had the company of a friend or other people when sleeping rough (Jones 1993b).

The respondents to the Homeless Survey were nearly all in the consumer group of single people in the labour force (91 per cent were single). This, following the discussion above, handicaps their entry into the housing market, since most housing caters for families, and there is no clear niche in the housing market for young workers. But most of them are currently unemployed or on training schemes, and very few are in full-time work. While some homeless young people were on Youth Training or receiving DSS benefits, others had no recognized income. In the previous chapter we saw that only one-third of homeless young people had received any recent financial help from their parents. Those under 18 years of age were therefore living on component incomes from training allowances, or severe hardship payments (if they were under 18 and could prove their case). These incomes, even with Housing Benefit, do not support independent living or the cost of setting up home.

Housing and homelessness careers

Homelessness does not necessarily occur when a young person leaves home, but may occur later, after a period in the housing market or more likely in insecure housing at its margins. Some homeless young people have thus never gained a foothold on the housing market, while others have fallen off the precarious footing they had. Current homelessness may be only one part of a housing and homelessness 'career', which may have involved an individual entering and leaving the housing market several times. The need for research to examine the processes involved in homelessness has been highlighted by Randall (1988) and Hutson and Liddiard (1991)[1]. The terminology employed here – *housing* and homelessness career – is intended to indicate that instead of seeing 'homelessness careers' as a downward spiral into long-term homelessness (see Hutson and Liddiard 1994), we should consider homelessness in the context of housing (and indeed households), as argued elsewhere in this book.

An analysis of the different addresses since leaving home, indicates that currently homeless young people had lived in a limited range of tenure types (Table 6.3). Much of the owned or council rented housing was in fact parents' addresses, returned to by many at first, though to a lesser extent as time elapsed. The longer since leaving home, the more complex the housing career, and the more likely it was to include living in hostels (as Hutson and Liddiard, 1991, 1994, have also found). Around 10 per cent of homeless young people slept rough at each stage; others may have slept rough at other stages. At the survey cut-off point in a long housing

Table 6.3 Housing and homelessness careers, Homeless Survey

Type of accommodation	1st %	2nd %	3rd %	4th %	5th %	6th %	7th %	8th %	9th %	10th %
Owned or rented – parental	21	12	6	8	5	11	8	7	6	7
Owned or rented – other	37	26	22	22	16	23	17	23	12	7
Bedsitter, student or nurses hostel	6	5	3	3	1	3	2	2	6	4
Institution (prison or hospital)	2	1	2	3	–	2	2	7	6	7
Homeless (inc. hostels)	26	47	52	51	64	56	62	58	67	70
Other and unclassified	9	8	14	13	14	5	9	2	3	4
All (= 100%)	230	193	161	107	80	64	52	43	33	27

Source: Homeless Survey 1992

and homelessness career, people are likely to be in hostels, council rented accommodation, prison, or sleeping rough, probably also forming a more distinct group of long-term homeless. Hostels did not necessarily end a homelessness episode, however. Some people had been evicted for breaking hostel rules, or had to move on because the hostel only provided emergency accommodation. They might then end up sleeping rough again. The types of behaviour which led to eviction from the parental home in some cases, might also lead to eviction from a hostel (see also Hutson and Liddiard 1994).

When asked how they last became homeless, young people tended – not surprisingly – to supply the precipitating factor rather than an analysis of underlying reasons. Homelessness here was frequently defined narrowly and equated with rooflessness. They became visibly homeless either from their parental homes, or from 'intermediate households' such as hostels and situations in which they had been hidden homeless. Homelessness also occurred after known temporary housing options had been exhausted, and in some cases as a result of migration to an unfamiliar area. Thus, conflicts at home are cited as a cause of homelessness as well as of leaving home, perhaps because they continue to affect a young person's relationship with their parents and prevent any prospect of returning home again even in an emergency.

Eviction was not only by families, though, and homelessness not always so closely related to leaving home. Thirty-two people became homeless when they were evicted from a variety of other accommodation, including digs, furnished flats, their own council flats, hotel accommodation, and hostels. One 'got barred from a cold weather shelter', while another said: 'I was drunk and started fighting with another resident in the hostel; I got thrown out'. Some young people appear to have done the rounds of the available housing and simply run out of options: 26 became homeless because there was 'nowhere for them to go'. Thus, 'friends would not let me stay any more' and 'no-one wanted me'. One specified: 'I had stayed with everyone I knew for a couple of nights and did not like to ask again'. This is the kind of insecurity meant by the term 'hidden homelessness'. Some could not get help from the council and had nowhere else: 'I had nowhere to go, council would not help me, Stopover was only temporary accommodation – nothing else'. One reported that there had been 'no room in any hostels as they were full, and my mother would not have me back'. Three had nowhere to go when they left prison. Nine became home-less when they moved to a new town and could not get accommodation there.

These subjective 'explanations' covered the most recent experience of homelessness, but some young people had been homeless more than once. In their Welsh study, Hutson and Liddiard (1991) found that the majority of young people they interviewed had been homeless more than once. Our own data on housing histories showed that 25 per cent of those currently in accommodation for homeless people had experienced more than one episode of 'extreme' homelessness in which they had slept rough or lived in accommodation for homeless people, interspersed with episodes in which they lived in other types of accommodation, when they may have been 'hidden homeless'. Eight per cent had experienced three or four episodes of homelessness. (One 'episode' in this sense may consist of several differ-ent 'addresses'). Sixteen of the long-term homeless became homeless after leaving their parental homes for the second or third time, and two of these had left home three times, becoming homeless on the last two occasions. This suggests that returning home is not a solution to the problem of homelessness even for those who can return: the problem may as previ-ously indicated simply be temporarily hidden, to reappear again later.

Of those sleeping rough, 23 per cent had previously done so (and indeed 23 per cent went on to sleep rough in their next situation). This would indicate that there has been no successful intervention, to prevent their continuing rooflessness. Thirteen per cent of those sleeping rough had previously been in a young person's hostel, while a total of 19 per cent had been in other forms of temporary accommodation catering for homeless people. Hostels may often provide a temporary *respite* in a career of homelessness, rather than *intervention* to prevent it.

Some individual housing and homelessness careers

See, when you sleep rough, you sit there and think of everything you've done, you dae. You think of all the bad things you've done and all the good things you've done. But you dinnae think of what you're gonna dae next because you dinnae ken. (Denise)

Earlier, this chapter considered the ways in which households may form as a deliberate strategy to affect housing market position. Homeless young people also move between different types of household but any strategies which emerge are more immediate and more crisis-based. As Denise indicates above, planning is difficult for those who are sleeping rough. Some brief 'case studies' are given below to illustrate some of the patterns in housing and homelessness careers. These are derived from self-completion questionnaires in the Homeless Survey. No pseudonyms have been allocated because the responses to the survey were anonymous. Housing and homelessness careers may include returning to the parental home (17 per cent of homelessness careers involved returns home, as in Case B), living in intermediate households, arguably as hidden homeless (28 per cent, as in Cases B and E), living with partners (12 per cent, as in Cases A and B), and living in hostels (as in Cases C and E).

Case A had a brief experience in the housing market, with a partner, before becoming roofless, rather than returning home. The question is whether her current accommodation in a young person's project will enable her to enter the housing market, or will she become longer-term homeless?

Case A

Female, aged 16, single. Unemployed for 6 months since leaving school. Lived with both parents until 16. Left home 5 months ago, because did not get on with parents. Became homeless on leaving home and has been homeless ever since. Gave 3 addresses:

1 At 16 lived with partner and someone else, in council rented flat. Left when partnership broke up.
2 Slept rough for over a month (in winter) sometimes with friends, last time alone. Then found accommodation, with the help of the police.
3 Young person's accommodation project, with residential staff.

Will not return home to parents because does not get on with them. Wants accommodation with partner.

Case B has a complex history, covering a range of experience. His problems appear to have started when his partnership broke up, and since then he has had a range of experience as hidden homeless and sleeping rough, before moving into his current hostel. This may (or may not) enable him to obtain housing, unless he does manage to emigrate as he hopes.

Case B

Male, single, aged 22. Left school at 16. Unemployed for the last year, and in all for about 3 years. Brought up by parents and grandparents until aged 15, and still has contact with family. Father was unemployed when he left home at 16 and is unemployed now. Left home because he wanted to live with his girlfriend in a place of their own. Gave 10 addresses:

1 Lived with partner, in council rented. Left when partnership broke up.
2 Lived with friends, in council rented.
3 Lived with friends and someone else, in council rented. Left because did not get on.
4 Lived with partner, in council rented. Left when partnership broke up.
5 Slept rough, alone.
6 Returned to parents' home, council rented. Was there less than 6 months. Left to move into better accommodation.
7 Lived alone, council rented, but was evicted. Spent decorating grant.
8 Lived with friends, council rented, but left because did not get on.
9 Slept rough, with others, for a few days.
10 Currently in a hostel.

B says he has been homeless for $3^1/_2$ years in all, and continuously for the last 4–5 months, since he was evicted. Does not intend to go home to live with his parents because he does not get on with them. He plans to get work abroad.

Case C has lived in various types of temporary accommodation, but has been evicted from several of them. There is a degree of circularity in his housing career. He has not, however, returned to his father's home. He says that he has never been homeless.

Case C
Male, aged 19, single. Left school at 14. Has done several Youth Training Schemes. Has been continuously unemployed for the last 2 years and has never had a full-time job. He was brought up by his father, who was in full-time work. He has 2 siblings. He left home at 16, because he did not get on with his father.

1 Lived alone, in council flat, but was evicted.
2 Bed and breakfast accommodation, and was evicted.
3 Bed and breakfast, left to go into better accommodation.
4 Young person's hostel, but was evicted.
5 Lived alone, in another type of housing, but did not get on with the people there.
6 Lived alone, in a temporary furnished flat. Left to move into better accommodation.
7 Supported accommodation project, for the last year, found through the housing department.

Does not consider that he has been homeless. He has never slept rough. He does not plan to return home to his father because there is no room for him. He wants a job, and a place in a shared flat, with support.

Case D was in care. He has never had a place of his own. He has been hidden homeless, but does not count himself homeless now that he is in a hostel.

Case D
Male, aged 18 and single. Left school at 16 with qualifications. Part-time job after Youth Training. Never been unemployed. Currently in part-time work (4½ hrs last week). Brought up by mother for 15 years and still has contact. In voluntary care at 15, with foster parents, and remained in care for over 3 years. Social worker helped him find somewhere to stay when he left care, and he says he still gets regular help. Gave 4 addresses since leaving care:

1 Lived with relatives. Bedsitter in private house. Left because had to move on.
2 Lived with relatives. Bedsitter in private house. Had to move on.
3 Foster parents. Had to move on.
4 Young person's hostel. Had to move on.

Has been homeless for last few months, since leaving his foster parents. He does not count himself homeless now. He slept rough, with a friend, for a while about 2 years ago. He does not know his parents' present circumstances. He wants a flat on his own and a good job.

Finally, Case E, aged 18, was also in care, but has since moved around so much that she has lost track of her housing and homelessness career. Most of her experience has been living in hostels catering for homeless young people, or sleeping rough. She is pregnant.

Case E
Female, aged 18, 6 months pregnant and planning to marry. Left school at 15, without qualifications. Has done several Youth Training Schemes, but left the last one before the end. Has been unemployed altogether for 2½ years and has never had a full-time paid job. Comes from a very large family. Subject of care order because of sexual abuse at age 3, and remained in care for 12 years. Social work department found her somewhere to stay when she left care, at around age 16.

1 In care. Children's home. Says she was evicted.
2 Slept rough for more than 6 months, left to move into better accommodation.
3 Young person's hostel. Had to move on.
4 Accommodation project. Did not get on with the other people there.
5 Slept rough, with other people, for 2 months.

She then lived in 5 or more accommodation projects, leaving because she broke the rules, or did not get on with the other people, and finally to move into better accommodation. Currently, she is in a young person's hostel, and was helped to find it by her social worker. Says she has lived in hundreds of addresses. Last became homeless 2 months ago, because 'money going missing from my purse and pressure to get involved in prostitution'. Altogether has been homeless for 3 years. Wants to settle down in a flat of her own with partner and child.

Though some of the SYPS case study respondents had managed to avoid homelessness, or 'solve' (or defer) their housing problem by returning home (see Chapter 4), returning home is not a solution to homelessness in the above cases. Three of the people described here cannot return home: for one it would be dangerous to do so, but another does not know where his parents are, and another says there is no room for him at home. The other two originally left home because of conflict with their parents and the relationship has not improved. It is worrying, however, that hostel accommodation appears frequently to be one step in a housing career which could contain further episodes of homelessness. A cycle of homelessness can easily develop if no effective intervention occurs, and the longer someone is homeless, the more damaging the experience is likely to be and the more difficult it will be for them to regain full participation in society. It is not just housing that is needed, but also jobs which would enable them to maintain an adequate standard of independent living even if housing were available.

Some of the new initiatives are beginning to recognize that the needs of young people are broad-based. There is recognition that the 'no home – no job' poverty cycle must be broken, and employer initiatives are increasing alongside housing ones (Employment Department 1993). The new 'foyer' initiatives will provide housing for single young people in the labour force within a package of guidance and support, and the intention is for secure and long-term 'move-on' accommodation to be available. The evaluation of the pilot projects is awaited with interest. It is only a pity that the foyer concept is based on a contract, described in the 1992 Conservative election manifesto's expression of support for the concept: 'We will carry out pilot projects for the foyer "concept", whereby young people are given a place in a hostel if in exchange they give a commitment to train and look for work'. Foyers thus risk becoming another manifestation of social housing targeted at the deserving poor. The initiative will fill one gap, but leave many others, including provision for those with partners, or in the process of forming partnerships, those with children (see O'Carroll 1992), and the most vulnerable, perhaps those leaving local authority care (see Morgan-Klein 1985).

When homeless young people were asked what would make their lives better in the future, many went further than to stress homes and jobs. They needed a secure home in the sense of a roof over their heads, the security that steady employment would provide, and other people, often in the form of a family of their own. Housing provision for young people must, therefore, allow family formation to occur.

Notes

1 Current doctoral research by Suzanne Fitzpatrick at the Centre for Housing Research, University of Glasgow, to be published in 1995, will fill an important gap in this respect. The research involves tracking and repeat interviewing a group of homeless young people. Interim findings suggest that young people who

have been in local authority care are more likely to become visibly homeless through presenting as homeless to agencies, rather than sleeping rough. This could indicate that official figures based on accommodation projects etc. may overestimate the proportions of homeless young people who have been in care.

Chapter 7
From stereotypes
to biographies

The argument in this book is that instead of trying to define patterns of leaving home as 'normative' or 'deviant', it would be more helpful to young people who are trying to make a transition to citizenship if we could consider the problems some young people face on leaving home in terms of 'risk'. We have seen that risk is part-structural, in that risk is unequally apportioned among young people, and partly an integral part of growing up, asserting individuality and independence, and separating from the relative security (in most cases) of the family home. Not only is risk unequally shared, but the ability to cope with it varies too. Strategies of risk reduction and risk avoidance have been considered. In the course of these discussions, we have caught glimpses of individual lives. This chapter introduces three biographies, which begin to summarize and illustrate the book's main themes.

The SYPS follow-up interviews were intended to provide data on how a group defined as being at potential risk in the housing market may have been able to develop strategies to avoid or reduce it. In previous chapters, data from these interviews have thrown light on patterns of leaving home, and strategies for accessing family support in order to return home, or gain material and financial help for setting up home. These findings have been presented as themes. In this chapter, we shall look at some individual biographies which reveal how risk developed and was, or was not, dealt with. The stories presented are those of Charlie, Patricia and Amy, reconstructed from the SYPS survey data and the follow-up interviews. These three have been chosen because they illustrate how young people manage to forge their lives within an unequal opportunity structure, the strategies they develop to mobilize their personal and family resources and thus improve their life chances. They also illustrate very different experiences, both of family life and the housing market.

Charlie appears to have had risk thrust upon him. He was excluded from family life as a child and subsequently left home because of his step-mother. He has been homeless, but not returned home or received much family help. He is unemployed and dependent on state benefits. Patricia and Amy, on the other hand, left home in order to become independent in the knowledge that this involved risk and uncertainty. Both have also been unemployed, and have had many problems in the housing market. In contrast to Charlie, though, they have not been entirely dependent on state support, but seem to have been able to mobilize family resources to reduce risk, Patricia in returning home to live, and Amy by obtaining housing through relatives. The importance of trust as a basis from which to take risks and cope with uncertainties comes out through these biographies. Patricia and Amy both knew that they could turn to their families if they needed help. Charlie had no such security.

Through these 'risk' biographies, we shall learn of the problems of becoming independent in youth, and the ambiguities which can arise during the transition to independence; we shall also hear of the feeling of power-lessness many young people feel during their youth, and the futility of planning ahead in an insecure world. We start with Charlie, who seems to have little control over his own life, but bends to the inevitability of fate, which appears not to be on his side. We go on to hear the story of Patricia, who made some attempts to live independently, but ended up sacrificing her dependence for the sake of security in the family home. Finally we hear from Amy, who is determined to forge her own life against the odds, and who refuses to resume dependence. Of the three, Amy is the survivor.

Charlie's story

Charlie lives alone in independent housing. He has been homeless, but has never returned to the 'parental home', however this is defined in his case. He has received little support from his family. He is depressed.

Charlie believes that if his 'mum and dad had a been together, things would have been different', but they separated when he was 7. His two sisters stayed with his mother, and he wanted to as well, but he was sent to live with his paternal grandparents, because his father would have been upset to lose his only son. He lived with them until he was 14, and was quite happy there, though he comments that older people do not really understand children. When he was deemed old enough to look after him-self, at 14, he was sent to live with his father, apparently more for his father's sake than his own:

LG: *Did you want to move in with your dad?*
C: Aye.

LG: Why did you want to move in with your dad?

C: I felt he was awfy lonesome. When he came in from work, he just used to sleep, come in and sleep. Working and sleeping. He used to greet [be upset] when I used to leave him at night. Just feeling sorry for him. Maybe myself tae, but I was quite happy at my gran's.

LG: So you moved in with your dad?

C: Mhmm.

LG: How long did you stay there?

C: About two year, until I was about $16^1/_2$.

LG: And when did it start going wrong?

C: When he married my stepmother.

Everything seems to have changed with the arrival of his step-mother, when Charlie was aged 15:

C: I don't know. It was just like an outsider coming in. And I just wouldnae dae what she tellt me. I just rebelled, started rebelling then.

LG: So did you leave or did you get thrown out?

C: Eh, well I kept threatening to leave. He says 'right, you've got two month to find somewhere else'. And she came in one night, and she said 'OK, man,' – I was in my bed and she switched on the lights – and I woke up and she says 'Check the state of him, he's oot his face'. And I hadnae even been on anything. So I got up and started going mad. So she came back in – 'You've got three weeks to find somewhere to stay'. I says 'Beat it, I'll leave in the morning'. So she put the light oot. So I just got up in the morning and left. Everybody was greeting, like, but I just had made up my mind. I dinnae go back on what I say, too proud, even though it's stupid.

LG: So did you like pack a bag?

C: Aye, just flung stuff into a poly bag, my claes [clothes], just stuck it in a launderette, and that was it.

LG: And where did you go?

C: Eh, this block of flats, slept on the stairs.

Charlie thus left home in a 'non-legitimated way', because of relationship problems. Retrospectively, he takes the blame. On balance, he felt, 'I would say it was my ain fault . . . I was drinking, smoking hash and that', though he said this was not the case the day he was thrown out. Leaving in an unplanned way, he had nowhere to go, and slept rough for several weeks. It was the worst time of his life: 'It was hard, cold and hungry'. He could have stayed at friends' houses, but did not want to 'impose', so when they asked him where he was living, he always said he was living somewhere else, and then went back to live on the streets. Altogether, he was homeless for eight months, until he was rehoused four years ago.

After his parents split up, he felt that his mother had abandoned him. Influenced by his paternal grandparents, he blamed her for everything, and took it out on her: 'I used to ignore her in the street, in front of friends, and shout abuse at her'. It seems to have been entirely due to an ex-boss that he got back in contact with his mother when he was 17, and he gets on quite well with her now. He tells the story:

> C: Well, it was my boss, when I was working there. I had money at
> the time and I said 'What are you wanting for your Christmas?' She
> says 'Phone yer ma'. And at first I thought she was kidding, then
> I picked up the phone and just phoned her. My ma thought I had
> got the wrong number. She picked up the phone – I was like that
> 'Are ye alright, mum?' 'Sorry, you've got the wrong number, son'.
> I was like that – 'I've no'. It was like that 'You have'. 'I've no,
> mum. It's me'. She just started greeting, so I went roond and seen
> her. Sorted it all oot.
>
> LG: *Was that not quite sad?*
>
> C: Aye, it wis. It was one of the touching moments.

By getting back in touch with his mother, he was able to hear her side of the story, and realised that she was not to blame. Unfortunately, this seems to have left him with no-one to blame but himself.

His housing career is fairly short. After the first period sleeping rough, he spent six months at his sister's house, but had to leave because there was not enough room for him. She kept wanting him to make it up with his father and go home. He kept going back to sleeping rough on the streets. He was not at first regarded as homeless by the Housing Department because there was room for him at his father's, however bad his relationship with his step-mother. The same ex-boss phoned the council every day until they gave him his present flat, four years ago. This was in hard-to-let housing, and had 'syringes on the stair and everything', when he first moved in. 'They just says if you're homeless and you're desperate you'll take a hoose. You cannae be choosy when you've no got nothing. It's a roof, it's better than staying wi' somebody else.' The block was done up two years ago and the other tenants rehoused, but Charlie 'didn't bother' to get rehoused. He says 'I stay maistly other places than I do here. I've never really liked this hoose, but it's just always somewhere tae come back tae.'

Charlie, in his high-rise flat, is depressed. 'I miss being with my family', he says, 'but then I couldnae live with my family', because he is too used to being on his own now. He has variable contact with his family, and says that they lecture him. He is currently unemployed, and has been for a total of four years. He goes out at night, but stays in during the day: 'Aye, that's what I mostly do, sit in watching telly. Sleep during the day. Try and sleep as much as possible.'

Given support when younger, Charlie may have been able to make better use of his own ability. He feels that he has wasted his life ('I've ruined my life in the last few years'). He 'had potential' at school, but got in with 'the wrong kind'. He truanted and became involved in glue sniffing.

Despite this, he obtained some qualifications and enrolled on a business studies course, but he gave it up because he 'couldnae get up in the morning'. He wishes he had stuck it out, but says he can't go back to the course now because he carried on collecting his grant after he left: 'I'd like to go back, but I cannae see me paying it off'. He never got back in touch with the college, though they asked him to, because he was 'too lazy. Just let everything build up. Instead of getting off my arse and daeing something I just sit aboot.'

He went on a Youth Training Scheme, as a plumber, but left after three weeks 'because all I was daeing was sweeping flairs. I dinnae think I was learning anything.' He became unemployed. Then, three months before his eighteenth birthday, he was affected by the 1988 change in social security regulations: 'they stopped my dole money so I had to take it as a YTS'. He found this 'brutal', because he was only getting £30 a week for working a full week, but was expected to pay £11.50 a week rent out of this. 'I went up to see them about that. And they says there was nothing they could dae about it.'

When he moved into his flat, his mother gave him a carpet, but he could not get help from the DSS, so he just had a camp bed for two months. He currently has debts of about £2,000, mainly for rent, Poll Tax and electricity. The electricity was cut off in the summer of last year: 'The bill was only for £93 and [when] the court put it back on through the Social, the bill came to £301. I dinnae ken. I was really annoyed at that.' The DSS are now deducting £11.50 a week from his income to pay it off. He also has bank debts.

Though Charlie appears to have been a casualty of family breakdown, he still feels that he is responsible for his current situation, but this feeling of responsibility is disabling. He appears to have sunk into a passive apathy. This extends even to his eating habits:

> I go days without eating ... You get over the hunger. You just get hungry and then you ken it's going to pass. Then when you get something you cannae eat it. It takes you a while to start eating again. Your stomach shrinks or something. A big plateful doon, and you're hungry and you start eating, you take a couple of moothfuls and you just say 'I'm no wanting it'.

Charlie seems to have 'coped' by resorting to drugs. He progressed from the glue sniffing to Valium and Ecstasy. This seems to have helped him 'see mair straight', and also to have become for once a participant in something, since he enjoyed the drug and rave culture. He still takes prescribed drugs, but has stopped taking Ecstasy. Occasionally, he sells drugs to get money. 'It's nothing to be proud of, but when you're only living on £16 a week it's hard tae survive.' Sometimes, he says, he feels he would be better off in jail ('That's you fed'), and sometimes he feels he is already in a jail.

He wishes he had got more help when he really needed it, as a child. This would include preparation for independent living, especially budgeting, but also emotional support. Looking back, he thinks the kind of housing he needed at 17 would have been similar to sheltered housing for the elderly, 'because it would have set you up, like going into yer ain hoose, but you would have someone there to help you out'.

Comment. Charlie has no plans for the future, or it seems the energy to put any into practice. His childhood experience, in which his needs appear to have taken second place to those of others during the separation of his parents and his father's re-marriage, seem to have left him with the feeling that his role is to be a pawn in the game of life, rather than an active participant. He has had few chances in life, and little capacity for choice. The apathy he suffers caused him to blow the chance he had at college. He lacks the ability to develop strategies for survival, unless his drug use can be counted as a short-term survival strategy. His apathy has further developed over time, as poor quality housing and dead-end schemes have not helped. He needed support and guidance. The most positive features of his life have been the employer who took an interest in him, and the renewed relationship with his real mother, which may over time repair some of the damage done to him. He appears to have been excluded from society in his high-rise 'prison'.

Patricia's story

Patricia has left home and returned twice. She did not receive family help for setting up home, though her parents willingly accepted her back. She has not yet achieved independence.

Looking back, Patricia also says her life has been 'a bit of a shambles', but reckons 'that's the way life is'. Her early problem appears to have been lack of self-esteem. She had a difficult time during her teens, and was bullied at secondary school for being overweight, but tried to look cheerful all the time: 'But I wasn't really. It was just a cover-up . . . I wanted to be with the in-crowd.' She left school at the minimum leaving age, without qualifications. She went on 'a few YTSs', which, like Charlie, she describes as 'complete slave labour'. At the end of her second YTS, she was replaced by another trainee and became unemployed. She says of YTS:

> If there's a job for you there, you should get the money. You should get the full money that everybody else is getting . . . You end up getting all the shitty jobs like cleaning the floor and cleaning the toilet . . . I'd hate to have to do it again. I'd hate to have to be forced like you are now [since the 1988 changes in DSS regulations], because when you're forced at that age – you're forced all the way through your life to go to school, then you're forced to go on this. You've no choice in your life at all.

She was unemployed for two and a half years, but is now working again, in a shop.

She comes from a 'close' middle-class family. Her father is a retired naval officer, currently doing a college course, and her mother is in part-time work. Several members of the family, but especially her mother, are members of a strict religious sect. Patricia and her mother used to be 'like chalk and cheese, arguing all the time', but 'we get on brilliant now'. Her father has always been too busy to have much time for her, and still treats her as a 'daft wee girl'. She is the fourth of five children. She and her older sister shared a room, until her sister got a boyfriend, and Patricia felt excluded and jealous. She was also at that time refusing to go to her mother's church, feeling she was being forced into something she did not want to do. That was when she decided to leave home: 'I just wanted to get right out, and find out I can handle the world myself, I want to go and do my own thing.' She decided that she had to take the risk and leave, but now says that this was a mistake. If she could re-live her life, she says:

> I wouldn't have moved out of my mum and dad's house. That was the worst mistake I ever made. I would have stayed here. But at that time there was no stopping me. It was 'Get out my way. I know what I'm doing. I'm so grown-up. I'm seventeen.' Well, I was nineteen or something. But I would have stayed here.

Later in the interview she says there should be places where young people can go and live for a while, and then go home again. Of her own experience, she says 'I wanted just a bit of freedom so that I could make my own choice, but my choices were being made for me'.

> I wanted to say 'Right, OK, I'll make that decision.' And most of the time it was the wrong decision, and I learned from my mistakes, but if I could make that mistake myself that was fine. It was my mistake. I made it.

In Patricia's case, leaving home was a means of defining herself as an adult. Though she says leaving home was her mistake, in practice it was her experiences in the private rented sector of the housing market that made her regret leaving home when she did. She moved into a bedsitter (she knew the landlord), and her parents helped her move. She knew when she left home that she had the option to return if she needed to, because the 'pre-emptive negotiations' had been done ('If it doesn't work out, can I come back?' 'Of course you can come back. Your room's there'). The only job she could get was a part-time job in a night club, and she became involved with 'the wrong kind of people'. She says she was very gullible at this time, and had no preparation for independent living.

She stayed at the bedsitter for six months, but did not get on with the other lodgers because she was coming home at 4 a.m. and sleeping all day. She moved to another bedsitter. Then the club closed down and she became unemployed. She did not realise that her new landlord was operating a DSS fraud, with Giros for non-existent people coming to the house, until the police arrested him and the house was repossessed. She was evicted with three days' notice. For three days she tried to find somewhere to live ('I didn't want to go back to mum, because I wanted to prove I could do it'), but she was jobless and none of the private landlords would take DSS claimants, so she had no option but to swallow her pride.

> So three days, and I phoned my mum: 'Mum, gonna come over and get me. I've got to come home'. She said: 'Right, OK'. So I only had three days so I came home. Came in the car and collected me. And I sniffled all the way home: 'I don't know why I moved out the house. I hated it.' But it was quite good. So I just came back here and it was all secure again. I was in my mummy's arms, I felt dead good!

So she returned home. She says, 'It wasnae actually that bad coming back to stay here'. She had her meals cooked, and came to appreciate the home comforts. That was when she decided that she would leave home in a different way next time, saying she would 'get a nice job and save up money and get a flat myself and start it all again, and do it the way I should have done it'.

When she looks back she hates that year away, and wishes she had either come back home or met her boyfriend earlier. Her boyfriend has helped her gain a more positive image of herself. He lives in another town, and she eventually left her parents' home again, to go and live with him and his parents. Patricia and her boyfriend were both unemployed. There were no jobs around, so they hardly bothered getting up: 'Like, we would go and sign on and that was it, go back up the road, in fact we used to get called John Lennon and Yoko Ono, because we lay in bed all day and watched the telly'. After about a year of this, she decided the fun was over and it was time to get a job. She came home to her parents again and joined the Job Club, spending all day every day there. Her boyfriend thought she was stupid, but she kept persevering, writing over 800 letters and getting 250 replies: 'but at the end of it I'm saying "Well, I got a job out of it, and I'm now Assistant Manageress, so there"'.

Like Charlie, Patricia wishes she had been better prepared for the problems she has had to face in adult life:

> When you're in school . . . they teach you how to count apples on a tree . . . They don't teach you about real things. Because when you actually do get out there it's a nightmare. And you just don't realise how hard things are. Even like for three days on the Social, trying to get a Crisis Loan. You're sitting going 'Oh well, my Giro's not come through. I'll go and get a Crisis Loan.' Three days later you're going 'I cannot believe – this is a crisis, I've no food' and everything. And they don't teach you about that in school. You don't learn that it's gonna be really hard and things can happen to you.

It is curious that Patricia does not think that her parents should have prepared her for independent living, especially when she continually comments in a positive way about the way her family functions co-operatively. Family closeness is stressed. She quotes her mother as saying about boyfriends, 'you don't go out with one person in this family, you go out with the family'. It is possible that this family is too close, and makes it difficult for individuals to leave. She said that her father would tell her off like a child, rather than have a discussion with her. She does not go to her parents for advice, and says that this is difficult when you live in a large family.

It is the formal sources of advice and guidance that she criticizes, however. She wishes that teachers had more time to listen, and that schools would 'open your eyes to the Social', and teach money management, household budgeting, and the practical aspects of running a house. She is disparaging about the careers service, who, she says, send young people off on schemes, but do not really care ('they gave you some nice leaflets sometimes, that you could colour in when you went home'). She describes her experience with the DSS:

> I hated going to sign on. I was never the sort of person – I knew I was gonna get a job so I always got up in the morning, washed my hair, put makeup on and ironed my clothes. It didn't matter what they were like. I mean, I had old clothes, they were old but they were ironed and they were clean, and I would always go and sign on. And it was 'Good morning' but they never even lifted their head to you . . . And they've just no time for you at all. I hate it. I absolutely hate it. It's the most degrading thing that I've ever done in my life, having to go and ask for money because my Giro wasn't there.

Nevertheless, she says that her family have always been there if she needed them. 'When I was coming back and forward they've always let me sort of use the place as a hotel.' They helped out with some furniture and with money too, when she was away from home, but Patricia was trying to manage on her own at the time and thought that their offers to help her were an excuse for finding out what she was doing and interfering in her life. She currently pays them £25 a week for her keep. She has debts of around £800, to her parents, friends, to the council, and on a credit card.

After her two attempts to set up an independent home, Patricia is still living with her parents, and her boyfriend now virtually lives there too. They want to get their own accommodation together, but 'he's not in a well-paid enough job. He's a painter by trade and he just can't get any work.' They do not want to live in the town where his family home is, because it is not as good for bringing up children, but 'to get a job [here] he'd need to have somewhere to stay and he can't get somewhere to stay until he gets a job. So it's a Catch-22.' Patricia says that they may have to buy a house, though they cannot afford a mortgage, because the council waiting list is so long, 'and I'm really kicking myself for not putting my name down when I was sixteen':

> I don't want to wait for the next seven years ... But I'll put my name down now, and then in seven years, I mean, I don't know what's gonna happen in seven years. I could be unemployed. We both could be unemployed. We could have a couple of kids and we're out on the streets. So I'll put my name down now and if a house does come up, well fine, but that's how long the waiting list is.

She knows that she cannot get priority rehousing unless she is accepted as homeless or 'unless I'm pregnant, which I don't want to be to get a house, I mean I plan to have a family some time in my life, but not now so I can get a house'. The only other option, she says, is sub-letting, but that is 'extortionate'. Patricia says it is time for her to settle down and marry, if only they could get somewhere to live.

Comment. Patricia had some bad experiences of private landlords, and thinks she could easily have been homeless if her parents had not taken her back. In practice, it would appear that she may be 'hidden homeless' now. So far, she has failed to make the transition to adult independence and has been forced back into dependence on her parents again. This is partly because of the lack of good affordable housing, and partly because of the apparent reluctance of her family to let go. No wonder Patricia talks of lack of choice. Currently, her chance of establishing her independence from her parents is now tied to her future in the partnership with her boyfriend.

Amy's story

Amy has never been homeless, and only returned home very briefly. She has received a lot of family support. Unlike Patricia, she has resisted a resumption of dependence, though she has experienced similar housing problems since leaving home.

Amy's life has been 'pretty blank and boring' over the past few years. Her ambitions have been thwarted as well: 'Well, I haven't achieved much, not what I set out to when I left school. I was going to do this and that, I wanted to travel the world. I still have these ambitions – whether I'll ever manage to do them.'

She left school and home at around the same time, when she was sixteen. She obtained some school qualifications and went to college to do a secretarial course, 'which was really pitiful', and then had a part-time job for two years until made redundant. She was living in a bedsitter. 'And that was the travel plans out the window.' She has only had one full-time job as a clerical assistant, but left after a year because she hated the work and the people, and only stuck it that long because of the money. 'One day

I just took a half day and wrote to them and said I was never coming back.' That was two and a half years ago. Moving into and leaving flats, even leaving home the first time, has apparently been a case of making a quick decision and acting upon it: 'Like I say, I make these decisions. And if I make them that day, I always try to do them that day.'

She said that getting her independence was the best time of her life. She wanted a taste of living on her own. 'One day I decided I wanted to try living on my own', and she moved into a bedsitter. She was suddenly taking on new responsibilities – she felt she had always been protected, and had never even paid board money to her parents, though, like all the sisters she helped around the house, doing 'chores'. She had to get used to budgeting and she just got on as best she could.

> Well, everything was new. You had to do everything for yourself. And just pottering about on your own and being able to turn your music up as loud as you want. Nobody's going to complain because everybody else in the bedsits got their music on. I don't know, just that feeling that everything's new, you're in a strange place. It would take you a few weeks to get the room the way you like it. And even going down to the shops was an excitement! It doesn't sound very exciting, does it? No, I liked that.

Her housing career has consisted of a succession of five bedsitters, the first few of which she shared. She did not get on with her first room-mate, 'when you're sharing a room with someone and she's quite a stranger anyway, to live there until you get somewhere else is quite impossible'. They had a row and Amy moved out that day. Just like Patricia, she trusts her family to be there when she needs them (though she sometimes wishes they would not let her keep running back), and so she phoned home:

> So I just phoned my dad and said 'I'm moving'. 'When?' 'Tonight. Could you come and get me?' He said 'Oh, my God. Alright then'. But somehow or another, one of the girls from the flat had phoned the landlord. He came up and threatened to throw me out if I didnae move out, so it was just as well I did.

She returned to her parents' home for eight weeks. She describes her mother as like a sister 'she's one of my best friends', and she gets on well with her father too; he's 'got a dry sense of humour and it appeals to me. We sit and we just crack sarcastic comments off each other ... I don't even smoke in front of my dad because he always used to say he hated women smoking ... I've too much respect to do it'. She has brothers, and a twin sister: 'My mum used to dress us identical until we got to about eight or something and we formed opinions of ourselves. It was horrible, because everybody expected you to be the same and even think the same. I think we went deliberately our own ways to prove to everybody that we were two different people.' This assertion of her individual identity seems to be the key to Amy's history.

She did not start looking for somewhere else straightaway when she returned home because she enjoyed the home comforts at first:

The first couple of weeks it was too much a novelty to be back. I could just stick my washing in the automatic machine and never have to worry about buying the food. I was just going in the fridge and helping myself. My room was mine again. My room was still there for me, because all the stuff was back in it, and after a couple of weeks I thought, 'I'm getting too used to this'. Like when I went back I had every intention of looking for a place, but I wasnae in a rush. And then after a couple of weeks I said 'I'm getting too used to this'. So I looked for something else.

She was 'getting too used to being dependent on them again'. Where Patricia had sacrificed her independence and was still living at home, Amy was not happy at being dependent:

I just thought to myself: 'If I keep staying here and keep staying here' – because my mum and dad were a bit wrong in the attitude that they had. They never took any money off us. I mean, it was great haeing money all the time. I mean, you werenae rich but you had the money, you didnae have to worry about paying rent. I mean, they never even asked anything for the phone bill. And if you offered them it, they would say 'No, you're only 16, 17, and you need your money. You dinnae earn that much anyway.' And I used to think to myself 'God, this could just keep going on and on and on and on, and the next thing I know, I'll be 20, then I'll be 30, and I'll still be here, and I'll never be able to stand on my ain two feet'. So that was it.

She moved into a shared flat with a young mother and her baby. She complained to the landlord about damp and draughts, but he would not get the repairs done. After advice from the Citizens' Advice Bureau she confronted her landlord:

And he was like 'Oh, this is my house. You won't tell me how to run my property. You either pay for [the repairs] and pay your rent at the same time or you're out' ... So I moved. That was it. I moved that day as well. Left my bed and everything. A new bed. All my cups, my cutlery.

Despite these experiences in bedsitters, she considers herself lucky that she 'got places which were quite safe'. For the last year and a half she has been living on her own in a furnished flat which she rents from her aunt. Her family have helped her with 'bits and pieces'. Her grandparents live in the downstairs flat. She feels safe there: 'there's not much could happen to me, anything in here, especially with my family all roond me'. She has gained security at the expense of privacy, though:

Aye, well, I like it, because all the hassle I've had with landlords and
that, at least I know if I was ever in trouble, if anything happened,
I can always run downstairs. But at the end of the day, they've got
their own life and I've got mine. It can be a real pain sometimes. You
dinnae feel as though it's as private as what you would like it to be.
I pay my rent and come and go as I please, and at the end of the day,
nobody can tell me different. But it is nice.

She thinks the council should keep a list of approved bedsitters for young
people who need to leave home, so that they do not have to move into
'shoddy' bedsitters with 'shoddy' landlords.

She has not had much help with housing from the council. She says she
went to the housing department one day when she was sixteen, to get onto
the waiting list, and she ticked the areas she would consider living, but the
man 'laughed in [her] face' because she had chosen all the nice areas. 'That
was it. And I just says to him "Rip it up, rip it up. I wouldnae take one
of your houses". And I walked oot. But he laughed in my face.' Having
been brought up in a bad area, she was determined not to go back: 'Once
you're in these areas there's a stigma, a class – that's it . . . I suppose that
was one of the reasons when I first decided to leave home. I thought "I'm
sick of this. I'm sick of this". People treating you like you're a piece of dirt
because you live somewhere and it's not of your choosing.' Her parents
have since been rehoused in a better neighbourhood, and live five minutes
away.

Amy is impulsive and has a quick temper. The latter, she says, is a
family trait:

I'd say we all have a streak of quick temper, that's probably why we
have constant arguments. But they're no' the kind of arguments where
you walk oot the door, slam the door, dinnae phone them for a
couple of days. They're the kind of arguments you walk oot the living
room, go into the kitchen and then – just say it's my mum – she'll
come through and we're joking, but it's like we're arguing. She'll say
'Make me a cup of tea, please'. And I'll say 'You're no' getting a cup
of tea. I hate you'. But she knows I'm joking, and she's joking and
she'll say 'That's why I love you so much'. And that's it, it's forgotten.
We dinnae think anything aboot it. It's just the way we have always
been.

Thus, the many minor rows do not grow into major ones, and she per-
ceives her family as supportive: 'I don't know. Just they're always there for
me if I ever need to go to them with a problem, you know. If I'm really
desperate for money or advice.'

She says they nag her sometimes, particularly to look for a job. When
she first became unemployed she says she was lazy, hardly bothering getting dressed, because she did not want to face another day of joblessness
and having to ask for money. Now, though, she resents any implication

that unemployed people are lazy, because though she is still jobless: 'I'm never in here. If I'm no' up at the JobCentre, I'm up the town or going to my mum's, helping my granny – now I do.'

She thinks there is 'no point in getting a small, part-time job' because 'you would only get aboot the same as what you would get on Income Support, but you would have to pay your rent and that yourself, so at the end of the day you would actually be poorer. You really need to get a full-time job.' She had a full-time job when she first moved into the flat in her aunt's house, but became unemployed when she left it, and apart from a part-time job for a while, has been unemployed since. For the last few months Amy has been actively looking for work, and has also thought about doing a college course in human development or child care, as this might help get a job or at least a 'foot in the door', but she cannot afford it and does not want to ask her family for the money, because she has too much pride, and because it would take her too long to pay off a loan.

Amy is currently getting about £30 a week Income Support, of which half goes on her rent. She says she had to appeal to the DSS to get that. She also receives Housing Benefit and has had a crisis loan. She too has debts of around £2,000 (on a mail order catalogue, to the council for Poll Tax, and to the DSS). She thinks she should be getting about £5 more from the DSS than she does, and that she could just about manage then. When she was recently waiting for the DSS decision on a rent allowance, her rent bill was 'building up and building up' and she was sure that if she had not got the rent, she would have been evicted, even though it was her aunt ('Business is business'). If this had happened, she would have stayed with a friend rather than return home to her parents again.

Moving into independent housing has not been easy for Amy. She felt she had to cope, or give up and go home to her parents. She decided to cope. Amy's independence is now too important to sacrifice again. She wishes they had made her stand on her own two feet earlier:

> I think they've probably done too much for me, probably helped me more than what other people would have helped their children. I mean, they offer me money, they offer to try and help me to get a job, to look for somewhere, but I'm so independent I want to do it all myself. I don't want anybody turning roond and saying 'Do you remember we got you this flat?' or 'Who got you this or that?' casting it up to me. I'm not saying they would, but if there was any chance of that, I'm no' going to have that – what I get, I get myself. And that's it. Whether they like that or no', tough luck!

Comment. Amy has constantly stressed her need for independence from her parents, but there are some ambiguities in her story: she has a flat of her own, but shares the house with relatives and knows that she can call on them for help if necessary. Though she says she is in a business relationship with her aunt-landlady, she has been able to mobilize family resources to make up for the lack of housing opportunities for a young person leaving home on a low income. She is, however, an impulsive young woman, not naturally given to long-term planning.

Choice and constraint

Given the structure of housing supply, and the limited opportunities for secure incomes sufficient for young people to set up independent homes, young people find themselves somewhere along a continuum between choice, at one end, and constraint at the other. All three biographies described are at the constraint end of the continuum, facing extreme risk in the housing market. Two were able to adopt strategies to avoid homelessness. One could not.

Resource strategies

Following the terminology of Pickvance and Pickvance (1994a), we can think of the way Patricia and Amy both mobilize their family resources as 'resource strategies', through which Patricia was able to return to the parental home, while Amy was able to access independent housing. Both also received family support. Use of these strategies was not, however, unproblematic. The findings described in Chapters 4 and 6 indicate that not all young people have the right to return home, and also that returning home may only postpone rooflessness, rather than be a solution to it. Patricia and Amy both knew when they left home that they could return, because the negotiations to prepare this safety net had already been effected. It seems clear from the case studies that returning to the parental home is not always a viable option, or necessarily a way of avoiding homelessness. Furthermore, young people who are trying to assert their independence from their parents may not be willing to sacrifice it: Amy refused to but Patricia did. The question hardly arises for Charlie. Charlie does not have a clearly defined home: could he have returned to his grandparents, his father and step-mother, or his mother, even if he had wanted to? Who could he have negotiated a return with?

In all, returning home may be a means of avoiding rooflessness for some, but is not an option for all. Furthermore, it may mean simply the substitution of one set of problems by another set, by extending dependency and 'privatizing' the problem of homelessness.

Housing strategies

Bedsitters have featured in two of these accounts, and indicate the insecurity and inadequacy of much of this type of furnished rented accommodation, which nevertheless is all that most young people leaving home can afford. Even so, both Patricia and Amy had to share rooms with strangers, and this gave rise to problems, though as the last chapter indicated, flat-sharing can be seen as a strategy for improving young people's positions in the housing market. Amy now rents from her aunt. Patricia was thinking about saving up for a mortgage. Charlie refused to live in other people's accommodation – in 'intermediate households', on friends' floors, and 'chose' rooflessness, because he did not like to impose. Charlie has now been rehoused by the council.

The ways in which housing departments allocate housing on points systems mean that young people may seek public sector rented housing in a number of ways. Various 'strategies' are used, with varying degrees of hope:

- *Going on the council housing waiting list at 16.* Amy started to do this, but tore up the application. Many other respondents anticipated their future housing needs by getting their names onto the waiting list as soon as possible, when they were 16 years of age, knowing that they would have to wait several years for housing. Patricia wishes she had done so.
- *Keeping up the pressure on the housing department.* Some young people are more able to further their own claims for housing. Charlie, however, needed a mediator, in the form of his boss. The importance of mediators was referred to in Chapters 4 and 5.
- *Forming a partnership.* Some housing authorities give extra points to couples, but Patricia was not apparently aware of this. This is consistent with the idea that leaving home in order to marry is still the most 'legitimated' reason for leaving home and thus likely to receive support.
- *Getting pregnant.* Though pregnancy ensures housing points, it is too heavy a price to pay, according to Patricia.
- *Getting homeless points.* Charlie was eventually accepted as roofless and housed in sub-standard accommodation (a hard-to-let flat) as a result. Patricia was aware that she would get a hostel place if evicted by her parents, but thought this an inappropriate strategy.

The alternative, as Patricia saw it, was to wait for up to seven years for public sector housing, or to stay in the parental home and defer the move to independence, or, for those who are lucky enough to have jobs and no debts, to save up for a mortgage.

Each of these young people suggested ways in which the housing risks for young people leaving home could be reduced. Charlie would like to see more supported accommodation for young people like himself. Patricia advocates extending young people's opportunities for making temporary moves away from the family home, through the provision of temporary accommodation which would enable them to return home again. Amy, on the other hand, would like the council to keep a register of approved accommodation for young people, which would include bedsitters.

Chapter 8

Conclusions

> I have had a rough time in the past four years and would not like to
> see this happen again to anyone, and I hope that by filling in this
> questionnaire that it will make folk sit up and do something about
> homelessness in Scotland and to help the young people who have
> nowhere to go. Thanks for listening.
>
> (Respondent to Homeless Survey 1992)

The above comment was written on the back page of a self-completion
questionnaire by someone who was herself homeless. The aims of this final
chapter are to provide a brief summary of the main arguments and findings of this book and to discuss their implications for policy and practice
in Britain as a whole. While the chapter aims to make 'folk sit up and do
something', it is concerned less with short-term policy strategies for dealing with current homelessness, than with longer-term strategies for preventing homelessness in the future, through taking a more positive approach
to young people's transitions to citizenship. First, though, let us briefly
rehearse the main issues which arise out of this study of young people
leaving home in Britain.

Summary

The book has reviewed empirical research on leaving home and has drawn
on new empirical research. Findings on international and historical patterns
of leaving home have provided the rationale for new analysis of large-scale
national surveys, and findings from these surveys have been examined
more closely with transcribed interview data. A new survey of homeless

young people has been analysed against the backcloth of national surveys of young people who may or may not have had experience of homelessness. This multi-method approach has thrown light on the central issue – leaving home – from a number of different angles. The book has sought, however, to move beyond a purely empirical study, however wide-ranging, to understand 'leaving home' in a more theoretical way, since this provides a framework within which to consider leaving home in the context of other transitions to adulthood, and to explore homelessness in the context of housing.

Polarities

The book has argued that 'leaving home' has become overlaid with emotional and moral overtones, and as a result the central issue, the transition in youth to independent living, has become lost from view. The ensuing application of labels of deviancy and normality to patterns of leaving home hinder our understanding both of the process itself, and of any problems young people may subsequently face in the housing market. The result has been a polarization between those who blame the housing market and other structural factors, and those who blame young people themselves, for any problems which arise when young people leave home. The 'moral panics' which have begun to surround 'the underclass', including young people who have been excluded from the housing market, may be counterbalanced by the arguments of advocates for young people who blame 'the system', but what can this stand-off achieve?

Risk as an explanatory device

The apparent polarity can be reconciled. This book has proposed that we think of young people entering the housing market as being on a continuum of risk. Two factors can then be considered: the extent to which risks are unequally distributed across the social structure, so that those with the weakest market position are most at risk; and the extent to which risks can be avoided or reduced (and market position enhanced) through individual strategies of survival. This is not to forget that access to strategies is also unequal. This framework allowed us to investigate and begin to understand the relationship between leaving home and entering the housing market. Rather than conceptually marginalizing young people who are currently homeless as an 'underclass', we were able to think about how and why some people who have characteristics (individual, familial or situational) which would indicate susceptibility to risk in the housing market, may be able to overcome it. This avoids a mere rehearsal of the characteristics of homeless young people compared with non-homeless – an approach which can unintentionally lead to over-stressing individuals' responsibility for their own circumstances – and maintains a notion of process rather than seeing current housing market position and homelessness as fixed states (and 'the underclass' as a static group). In sociological terms this approach has involved integrating the often competing explanations of structure and agency, through the concept of 'reflexive biographies' (Giddens 1991; Beck 1992).

Case studies were used to examine the circumstances in which strategies might be used as a means of reducing or avoiding risk. The strategies identified related to finding ways of returning home (Chapter 4), accessing family support for setting up home (Chapter 5) and improving one's position in the housing market (Chapter 6). It seems clear from this study that not all young people can mobilize resources in this way. Some feel powerless to direct their own lives, and even those that do appear to use strategies may not overcome structural constraints. Those returning home because they had nowhere to live, for example, may only be hiding or deferring their housing problems.

There are some people who may face the greatest risks, and be least able to avoid them. These include young people suffering the effects of parental conflict or family breakdown (including many of those leaving care), and those from families experiencing unemployment and poverty, or deprived areas where there are no local opportunities for work, training or education. Some implications for policy and practice in respect of young people leaving care, and leaving families because of conflict, are discussed below. The needs of young people leaving home in deprived rural areas are the subject of current research by the author (with Lynn Jamieson). It has been beyond the scope of this book to consider young people with other special needs, such as those with disabilities. However, the framework developed here can be extended to include patterns of transition of young people in other such groups.

Social construction of legitimacy

It is argued here that because the rights of young people to housing are problematic, access to housing tends to depend on the socially-perceived legitimacy of their claims. Thus the transition out of the parental home is more likely to receive support when the reason for leaving home (and the age at which someone leaves) is perceived to be within the contours of 'normality' and 'tradition'. Chapter 2 considered how social legitimacy may be constructed on the basis of false assumptions about 'traditional' and normative patterns of behaviour. Leaving home, being an integral part of the broader transition to adulthood, is affected by the structures not only of the housing market but also of education and training, welfare, and employment, which also affect family formation and transition into the labour market. Patterns of transition out of the parental home are therefore subject to change as participation in education and training extends, as the labour and housing markets change, and as family formation is delayed. Comparison of current patterns with those in the past and in other countries indicated the extent to which they are affected by the social structures and institutions of the time or the countries concerned (Chapter 2). Some aspects of leaving home in current Britain which we may consider new have their roots in centuries of practice, while 'traditional and normative' patterns have relatively modern origins. For example, intermediate households (between parental and partnership households) played an important part in patterns of leaving home both a century ago and now, while the 'normative' patterns of direct transition from the parental household to the marital one derive most obviously from the 1950s and 1960s.

Intellectually and logically, we can probably agree that there is no such thing as a 'normative' pattern of leaving home. However, the moral panic which has attached to homelessness has extended to young people leaving home, such that leaving home 'too soon' and for the 'wrong reason' are seen as deviant, and, as Chapter 3 revealed, associated with a higher *risk* of homelessness. These images have been internalized by young people themselves, and in retrospect they speak of 'the right way' and the 'right time' to leave home (Chapter 3), thus adopting the normative model in theory if not in practice. If support for leaving home depends on the social legitimation of the timing and reason for leaving home, young people leaving home in 'deviant' ways are less likely to receive support either from the state or from their families, though they are the home-leavers most likely to need help.

Current patterns

Chapter 2 showed that in recent years young people appear to have been leaving home earlier, but also that more have been returning home to live with their parents again. This changing pattern was explored in the following chapters. This is a new and important finding, not reflected in previous research because, it is argued, research has tended to focus on the last leaving home event rather than the first one. It seems that returning home has been overlooked by research because of the limitations of the data available, and because of an assumption that leaving home (being mainly associated with marriage) was a one-off event. In any case, returning home has become more common in the last decade. The significance of this finding is that it suggests that the level of housing demand among young people may have been greatly underestimated. The increased incidence of returning home suggests that leaving home has become more difficult.

Recent change is also significant in other ways. Government policies tend to be based on a model of economic rationality, whereby it is assumed that young people should leave home only when they can afford to do so, and therefore that policies removing the 'incentives' to leave home will have the effect of keeping people at home for longer. The previous chapters have indicated that neither leaving home nor young people's housing demands can be regulated in this way. Young people are not always able to choose the most appropriate or viable time to leave home, though they may have clear ideas later about the economic viability (or not) of leaving when they did (Chapter 3).

An examination of the current patterns of leaving home in Britain (Chapter 3) showed that many of the younger home-leavers leave because of constraints, such as family conflict, family poverty, or because of the limitations of the local labour market. These young people often have little choice about the timing of leaving home, and they may not be prepared for independent living or able to afford it. Indeed they indicated (Chapter 5) that they grew up and became more adult as a result of leaving home. 'Normative' patterns of leaving home are more likely to be based on economic rationality, involving choice; marriage, going away to college, or taking up a job (elsewhere or with accommodation attached), may be more associated with choice, and thus more amenable to manipulation through government policies.

Increased housing demand

For many reasons, including the extension and expansion of higher education, delayed marriage and childbirth, and the wish of more young people to be independent, young people's housing demands have diversified. In particular, the demand for suitable housing especially for *single* young people has increased, since fewer young people leave their parental homes to move directly into partnership ones. Accommodation for single people is polarized between housing catering for the wealthy, and insecure 'transitional' housing for the young single person. The availability of affordable accommodation has decreased. One result of this is the increase in youth homelessness over the last decade. Another is the increase in numbers returning home after apparently failing to establish an independent home (Chapter 4). Whether or not demand for housing can be reduced through state regulation (for example through social security regulations) of leaving home depends on the extent to which leaving home is a matter of choice or constraint, and also whether returning home is an option for young people. The book argues that the tide of young people seeking independence in youth cannot easily be turned, though they may recognize the risk of homelessness. Taking risks and facing risks are means by which young people assert their independence and establish their ability to survive (Chapter 3). This is not the same as to say that young people are homeless because they want to be.

Support for setting up home

The extension of education and training, the withdrawal of employment opportunities and the welfare safety net from young people, means that they remain in a state of dependence for longer. Policies have been based on an expectation that middle-class patterns of family support can operate in working-class families in two respects: the opportunity to return to the family home (Chapter 4) and access to family economic support (Chapter 5). These assumptions are erroneous too. It is assumed in both cases that by restricting state support to young people, middle-class practices of extended family support can be adopted and practised in working-class families whose class culture involves different forms of family support. In working-class families, the normal practice has been for young people to bring money into the household budget rather than take money out of it. Economic support in working-class, and indeed rural, families is less likely to take the form of financial help. The withdrawal of state financial support from young people making the transition to adulthood has resulted in many more young people having to seek family help in these respects despite there being no tradition that they do so.

Returning home has also been less common in the past for young people from working-class families than it has for middle-class ones. While students have often followed a practice of returning to their parental homes for vacations or when their courses are over, young people from working-class families were more likely to be leaving home to marry and therefore less likely to return home. Chapter 4 argued that young people have no automatic right to live with their parents, but do so with their parents' consent. This consent may be affected by differences in social class expectations. Further research is needed to explore this point. It seems, however, that returning home depends for many on there being an invitation from the parent for them to do so. Evidence was provided both in a national survey and in-depth interviews.

Access to family financial support clearly varies according to social class. It also varies according to family relationships (Chapter 5). Family support does not, therefore, conform to a clear model of economic rationality any more than does leaving home or returning home: even where young people need economic help and their parents are financially able to provide it, it may not be forthcoming. It is not only in poorer families, but also in families where there has been conflict, that family support may not be available to make up the deficit left by the withdrawal of state support. Young people who have left home because of family conflict are particularly vulnerable, as they are the least likely to have access to support from either their families or the state. Furthermore, an extension of dependency or a return to dependency may not be acceptable to many young people who seek independence. Complex negotiations may be needed to access support in a way which is acceptable to all those involved. More research is needed to understand the ways in which young people may or may not be able to access family support in wealthier middle-class families, for example, since it is unclear whether these concerns about an extension or resumption of dependence would affect middle-class young people in the same way, or whether they may find it easier (because of different class cultural expectations and patterns of longer periods of dependency) to ask for help.

It is ironic that several of the young people quoted in Chapter 5 indicated that their relationships with their parents improved when they left home. Access to family support may therefore improve over time, as young people move beyond adolescence and develop a more equal relationship with their parents. Until a more equal relationship is achieved, it seems that young people will resist the resumption of dependency which asking for parental help would entail. Further research is needed to show whether these findings can be generalized to other young people, all of whom are likely to be trying to assert their independence and prove that they can cope without parental help. It seems, though, that it is the younger home-leavers who most need help, but who are also the least likely to receive it, either from their parents or from the state.

Housing and homelessness

Young people's housing needs must be understood and recognized. The concept of housing careers reflects underlying dynamics (Chapter 6). Young people entering the labour market need flexibility in their housing, to be able to move in search of work, or to follow employment careers. Those from deprived rural areas moving into more favourable labour markets need to be housed, for example. But the dynamics inherent in youth are not restricted to employment and work careers: there is also the question of family formation. While young people leaving home initially need accommodation as single people, there needs to be an additional flexibility, to allow household careers to develop, so that the single person can form a partnership and gain access to a partnership home. Flexibility, therefore, needs to be considered in geographic terms, to allow geographical mobility, and also in terms of housing type, to allow the development of partnership homes.

The rigidity of the current housing market means that many young people have problems obtaining appropriate housing, and some become homeless. The link between leaving home and homelessness is not always a direct one, and many people become visibly homeless after a period of time in housing other than their parental homes, because they have lost their homes (for example, through fire or eviction), or because they were in unsuitable or insecure accommodation (such as 'hidden homeless') in intermediate households (Chapter 6). Homelessness on leaving home is most likely to occur when someone has had little choice about the timing of leaving home, and when the reason for leaving itself represents constraints (such as that they could not have stayed, rather than that they felt ready to move into independent housing). This is why some 'characteristics' (reflecting risk positions) common to early home-leavers and to homeless young people are significant: for example, the incidence of family breakdown, unemployment, and experience of local authority care (Chapter 3).

It is important to examine the housing and homelessness careers of young people (Chapter 6), and more research is needed. Not only does this allow greater understanding of how people become homeless, but it also indicates how or whether homeless people gain or regain a foothold in the housing market. Instead of thinking about an inevitable downward spiral into 'the underclass' of long-term homeless, it is more relevant to consider the effectiveness of support agencies, hostels or returns to the family home in intervening to prevent further homelessness. And even more profitable to think about how even short-term homelessness could be prevented, if young people leaving the parental home were enabled to gain access to suitable accommodation.

Implications for research

This book has attempted to clarify the subject of leaving home as an area for research, and has highlighted some of the definitional problems involved. It also indicates the need for further research, for example on the effects on family life of increased parental responsibility for young people, and of the increase in returning home. Research is needed on social class variation in current patterns of support, and differential access to living in the parental home. This research should move beyond considering what happens in families experiencing poverty and family breakdown (such as reported here, or in Allatt and Yeandle 1992, and Hutson and Jenkins 1989) to considering intact and wealthier families. Following the lead of these commentators, some of this research should consider the parents' accounts as well as those of young people. This indicates the need for a further move in research towards considering young people's situations in the context both of their families and of the wider social structures, and thus further integration of the sociology of youth with that of family life.

More recognition is needed that leaving home is a process and not necessarily a one-off event: returning home should be seen as a part of the process. This means that studies of leaving home should define whether they are examining first leaving home, last leaving home, or a mixture of both. Cross-sectional studies based on current household composition, or any study based on inadequate definitions, will only confuse. At a time when young people are facing increasing problems as they try to become independent, it is important that policy makers and practitioners should have access to research which is as well-defined and accurate as possible, so that the most appropriate solutions can be found.

There is, therefore, a clear case for longitudinal studies, whether surveys or the tracking of individual case studies, in order to understand the processes involved in leaving home and returning home, and in housing careers, whether or not these involve homelessness. The SYPS, which has provided most of the quantitative data on which this book was based, as well as the sampling frame for the qualitative case studies, was discontinued in 1993. Current large-scale longitudinal studies which could, but do not, include questions of leaving home and entry into housing are the new Scottish School Leavers' Survey, which replaced the SYPS, but focuses on education and training, and the Youth Cohort Study in England and Wales, which is similarly focused in scope. Both provide a framework which could be extended to allow the continued study of leaving home in Britain.

Implications for policy and practice

The findings described in this book seem to have clear practical and policy implications, but it is beyond the scope of the book (and its author) to make specific recommendations for action. I can only indicate some areas where I believe further consideration, or action, to be needed. There are first some specific issues, relating to particular social groups, such as early school-leavers, young people in families experiencing breakdown, and those leaving care. There are also broader issues which need to be taken into account when considering social policies affecting young people as a whole, issues concerning housing and income needs in youth, and the need for a whole new approach to young people which puts their needs before those of the economy or 'the system', and which begins to identify ways in which young people can be better supported through the transition to adulthood. These are considered in turn.

Early interventions

The research indicates the need for early intervention, perhaps through schools, not only to provide support for young people who need it, but also to provide more guidance and preparation for adulthood. This applies particularly, though not exclusively, to young people who leave school at the minimum age, and those who truant before it. Several of our interviewees said they wished they had received more help before they left home, to understand about housing and social security systems, for example, or to learn how to budget and pay bills (see for example the biographies in Chapter 7). They recommended talks in schools, given by outsiders such as people from social security or housing departments, on what is available and, more importantly, what is not. The people who need such guidance are likely to be precisely those who gain least academically from schools, and who have the least positive relationships with their parents – in other words, the ones who are most likely to leave home when they are ill-prepared for independent living.

Leaving home packs, such as those developed by Glasgow City Housing, Shelter and Centrepoint are another way forward and are becoming more common. The better young people understand the constraints and limitations (as well as any opportunities) *before* they leave home, the more they are able to negotiate them, including, where appropriate, by deferring leaving home.

'Respite' care

Many younger home-leavers in particular leave because of family conflict, because their own relationship with a parent or step-parent has broken down. Often this is associated with family reconstitution and the presence of step-families. The combination of leaving home when relatively young (and thus in a poor market position) and having a poor relationship with parents (and thus reduced access to family support) leads to particular problems in the housing market. While a relatively large proportion return home to live again (Chapter 4), some do not and may become homeless instead. The link between family conflict and homelessness has been clearly identified in this book, and requires further attention, but the policy solution may not be to put more pressure on parents and children to conform, which might only exacerbate the problem, but to find ways of supporting families in this situation.

Families may on occasion need respite care for their young people (as Maas, 1986, has indicated in the Australian case). This is an equivalent to respite care for elderly or sick people being cared for in their families. Consideration could be given to the provision of respite care to provide breathing space for young people and their parents alike; this may allow them to weather the crisis. This means that some young people could live away from home for a while until they felt able to return. It is similar to Patricia's proposal that temporary moves away from the parental home should be supported, and also, perhaps, to Charlie's suggestion of sheltered housing for young people (Chapter 7). During the initial period of separation, social workers could be involved in paving the way either for a return home until a more planned leaving can be effected, or for a move into more independent housing if a return home is not appropriate (if, for example, the young person would be at risk if they returned home).

Support for leaving care

This study, while not specifically about young people leaving care, does raise issues which concern them. Around one in three homeless young people have been in local authority care, and this frightening statistic, found in several studies, means that it is vital to understand why. On the one hand, young people leaving care face the same constraints as others in the education system, labour market and housing market. However, they appear to be handicapped in two ways in particular: first, they are not usually able to return 'home', once they have left it; and second, they may not receive sufficient or appropriate help for setting up home.

Leaving care should be regarded as a process equivalent to leaving the parental home. In this sense, young people leaving care should not be seen as necessarily having special needs, but simply as needing the same as anyone else. Young people leaving care may equally need to be able to regard their first move as a tentative one. This may be because of the insecurity of their housing and employment, or because they may not feel ready for independent living. Leaving care should, therefore, no more represent a one-way move than leaving many parental homes. The research indicates that thought should be given to the provision of facilities for care-leavers to return to an appropriate care environment if necessary. Young people leaving care may also need the knowledge that there is a safe haven (with support levels appropriate to individual needs) to which they can return.

Secondly, young people leaving care are often not in a position to seek financial help from their families. While current structures can and often do offer support, guidance and financial help to young people leaving care, the support provided is very variable, and may be based on narrow definitions of young people's immediate rather than longer-term needs.

A change of approach

'Doing something about homelessness' means more than providing housing, or catering for particular groups. It means understanding the needs of young people growing up to become independent citizens, and creating structures within which they can become financially independent, establish new households and form new families of their own. This means that employment, social security and housing need to be considered together, along with the provision of social support for those who need it, in what is commonly known as a 'holistic' approach. It further means that policies should be based on an awareness of 'process', and allow youth transitions to take place. At a general level, a positive, integrated youth policy would consider ways of helping young people become citizens by emphasizing their rights as well as their responsibilities, in contrast to current government policies which focus on social control and reduction of the social security budget (discussed in Jones and Wallace 1992). The need for greater communication between agencies in cases of specific need has also been advocated: in the case of young people leaving care (Morgan-Klein 1985) and in the case of teenage lone parents (O'Carroll 1992). Coles (1995) points out that 'special needs' groups also have needs in common with other young people making the transition to adulthood, but this can be overlooked.

There is a danger, however, that further integration of policies could lead to a further stress on social control, rather than social support (see Davies 1986). Young people need policies which allow them the scope to take on adult responsibilities, rather than policies which take away their scope for choice and force them to act in particular ways. An example of the latter is the linkage of incomes to training schemes for the under-18s, when many young people see no value in the schemes themselves, and when training allowances are at a level which effectively prevents a successful transition from the parental home.

Maintaining the concept of process

Supporting the transition to adulthood means, in policy terms, at the very least creating a housing market which has suitable accommodation for young people, and ensuring that their incomes are adequate to compete in it.

New initiatives are needed, however. Young people's demands on the housing market have increased at a time when affordable housing has become scarce. Moreover, the nature of young people's housing demands has changed, becoming more varied. That the current housing market does not cater for young people is evidenced by the large, and growing, numbers of young homeless. It is important not only that the housing and other needs of young people currently homeless should be met, but also that the problems of homelessness should be tackled at its various sources, that is in the structures which have reduced the competitiveness of young people in the market place.

Young people leaving home need a flexible youth housing market in which there is a range of housing appropriate to their current and changing needs. Flexibility is necessary because they may need to move to find jobs, they may form partnerships and families. Variety is needed because young people's current housing needs vary according to whether they want to live alone, with peers or in a family home of their own. The question is, how can an unregulated housing market provide accommodation to young people which is not only flexible and varied, but also safe and secure? One of the respondents, Amy, made one suggestion (Chapter 7): that local authorities should maintain a register of landlords offering safe private rented accommodation.

Youth incomes form the other side of the affordability equation. In order to be able to compete even within a reformed and broader youth housing market, young people need incomes capable of sustaining independent living. This applies to youth wages, but also to incomes from grants, training allowances and benefits. It is clear from the research described in this book that economic competitiveness cannot be guaranteed by families making up the difference between a youth 'component' income and a full adult income, because many families do not. Current income levels in youth often do not even take into account the living costs of young people living in the parental home.

The whole structure of income in youth needs investigation. It is hard to see how any progress can be made unless Income Support is restored to young people in the 16–18 age group. The age grading which forms the basis of social security benefit levels in youth goes completely against the idea of supporting transition, since age is a poor indicator of income need in youth. Training allowances, youth wages from work, and student incomes are all held at low levels, which appear to bear little relation to income needs in youth. This in itself is likely to increase the pressure on family relationships.

A 'holistic' approach

Increasingly there are signs that young people's difficulties in finding employment and housing are being linked and more 'holistic' solutions sought. These include the foyer initiatives (Chapter 6) in which the Employment Department and the Department of the Environment are involved, with other non-governmental organizations such as Shelter, YMCA, and London Quadrant Housing Association. They aim to create new provision for young single people in the labour market, offering guidance and support as well as short-term housing and move-on provision, for those willing to give an undertaking that they will work or train. There is a danger though that instead of providing much needed accommodation for their original target group, young single workers, the foyers are becoming perceived as the answer to youth homelessness, and too much may therefore be expected of them. There is also a danger that the foyer principle of getting people into work and move-on accommodation may be based on an assumption that transitions in terms of work and housing always involve progression along a single path. What happens, therefore, when someone loses their job, for example? And what happens when they want to live with partners? The evaluation of the foyers pilot projects by the Centre for Housing Policy at York University will soon be published.

Other initiatives are specifically aimed to help young people break out of the 'no home: no job' poverty trap. Two of these encourage employers to take on young homeless people, thus breaking the vicious circle of joblessness and homelessness. Recent employment initiatives for homeless people include LEAP (Linked Employment and Accommodation Project) and GATE (Guaranteed Accommodation and Training for Employment), which are beginning to take a broader approach, and in so doing, destigmatize 'the homeless' at least among those employers taking part in the projects (Employment Department 1993). There are also some 'social self-build' projects, through which young people are helped to build housing in which they will eventually live, again helping to redress common stereotypes about the homeless and making young people feel involved rather than excluded (Joseph Rowntree Foundation 1994a).

The holism needs to be extended, however, from looking at the needs of the currently homeless to providing for the needs of the next generation of young people who are about to leave home as part of their normal transition to adult citizenship. This is where foyers, as one part of a programme of initiatives to support young people's transitions to citizenship, have their place. Only by improving the economic position of young people, through jobs or realistic social security arrangements, as well as providing a range of housing options for them, can young people be helped to make a 'successful' transition to adulthood. Positive policies are needed. There really is no justification for creating a 'lost generation' of young people and then being frightened of them.

Appendix 1

Research projects, data sets and publications arising

This book is based on a programme of original research comprising the projects and publications listed below. Fuller details of each data set are given in Appendix 2.

1 Leaving the parental home

An exploratory study of leaving home and early housing careers formed part of my ESRC-funded doctoral research at the University of Surrey (Jones 1987a, 1987b, 1988). This was based on secondary analysis of data on the birth cohort of 23-year-olds in the National Child Development Study, 1981 (Shepherd 1985). The study is frequently referred to in this book for comparative purposes.

2 Household formation among young adults in Scotland

This short project, funded by Scottish Homes, involved secondary analysis of the Scottish Young People's Survey first cohort, surveyed in 1985, 1986 and 1987 at $16^3/4$, $17^3/4$ and $19^1/4$ years. This cohort is referred to in the book as the SYPS 1985/87. The research resulted in two publications: a full report published by Scottish Homes (Jones 1990), and an article on young people leaving home in rural Scotland (Jones 1992a).

3 Parent–child economic exchanges

The same SYPS 1985/87 cohort formed the basis for a brief study of young people's contribution to the domestic economy while living with their parents. (See Jones 1991 on the cost of living in the parental home, and Jones 1992b for a broader analysis of the economic relationship between young people and their parents.)

4 Young people in and out of the housing market

This two-year project, supported by the Joseph Rowntree Foundation, was conducted by the Centre for Educational Sociology with the Scottish Council for Single Homeless. It was based on two distinct sources of data: the SYPS second and third cohorts, referred to here as the SYPS 1987/89 and the SYPS 1989/91, and a purposive survey of homeless young people in Scotland (known as the Homeless Survey, 1992). Additionally, a subset of the SYPS cohort at age 21/22 years, and 63 homeless young people aged 16–22 years were interviewed for the project (see Appendix 2). The quantitative analysis in Chapters 3, 4 and 6 is based on this study, as well as the case studies in Chapter 7. A set of five project working papers gives full details and is available from CES or SCSH.

5 Family support for young people

This six-month project, also supported by the Joseph Rowntree Foundation, involved further analysis of the SYPS and the qualitative data from the SYPS case studies interviewed for the previous project (see Appendix 2). Chapter 5, and the qualitative analysis in Chapters 3 and 4, are based on this study. The qualitative data were analysed using the Ethnograph software package (Seidel *et al.* 1988). For fuller details see the research report, Jones 1995.

6 Current related research

Additionally, two projects are underway which develop the programme further. The first (with Denise Burns and Janet Siltanen) is a study of 'Income and Expenditure in Youth', a two-year ESRC-funded project, based on secondary analysis of the Family Expenditure Survey. This will consider the social adequacy of youth incomes during the transition to independent living. The second project (with Lynn Jamieson) is a two-year study of youth migration from rural Scotland. This is also funded by the ESRC. It is based on secondary analysis of the SYPS and follow-up interviews with a rural subset of respondents at 21 years of age.

Appendix 2
Data sources

The data sources used in the projects 'Young people in and out of the housing market' and 'Family support for young people' are shown in Figure A.1. The aim was to examine young people's experiences of housing and homelessness through integrating findings from a representative national survey of young people (the SYPS), with a survey of homeless young people (the Homeless Survey). This method allows us to consider homelessness as being at one end of a continuum of risk, rather than a separate phenomenon. Case studies were undertaken with the aim of understanding how risk occurred and how it might be avoided. The data sets are now described.

Scottish Young People's Survey (SYPS)

Survey data

The SYPS is a biennial national survey of young people in Scotland, conducted by the CES until 1993. The surveys include a series of four school year cohorts, on which all the SYPS analysis described here is based. The first cohort, SYPS 85/87, was used for earlier research on leaving home, as indicated in Appendix 1. The project 'Young people in and out of the housing market' involved secondary analysis of the 2nd and 3rd cohorts in the series, referred to here as the SYPS 1987/89 and the SYPS 1989/91. The technical reports for each survey give fuller details of sampling and data collection. For each cohort, a 10 per cent sample of young people was selected during their 4th (final compulsory) year at secondary school in Scotland, and surveyed the following spring at average age 16³/₄, and again

Figure A.1 Young people in and out of the housing market data sets

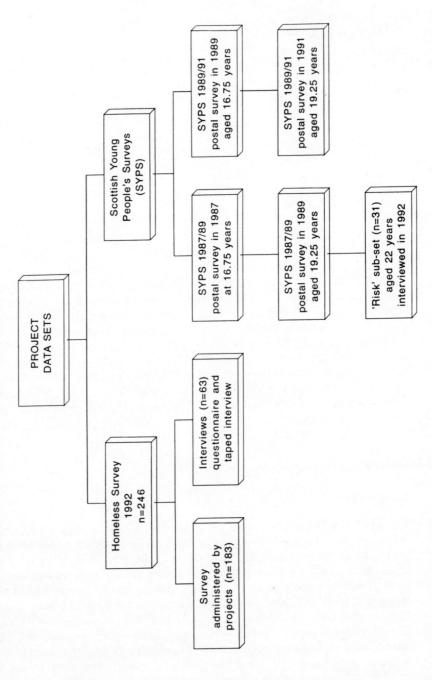

two and a half years later, in the autumn, when their average age was 19¹/₄ years. Response of around 80 per cent at the first sweep and 65 per cent at the second sweep, of the original target sample, gave an achieved sample of 4,447 and 4,019 respondents at the second sweeps of the two cohorts (Brannen *et al.* 1991; Brannen and Middleton 1994).

Case studies

For the project 'Young people in and out of the housing market', a subset of respondents to the SYPS 1987/89 was interviewed in 1992 at around 21 years of age. The case studies were selected on theoretical grounds. From the survey data, we selected a subset of people who had left school at or near the minimum age and left home by the second sweep of the survey, and therefore had experience of the housing market other than as students. Further criteria were:

• evidence of family breakdown OR father's unemployment
• OR evidence that the respondent had experienced unemployment.

These criteria were imposed because they were found from the survey analysis to be indicators of risk in the housing market. The aim was to explore strategies through which people who faced risk may have managed to avoid it (see Figure A.2).

The subsetting procedure produced a sampling frame of 345, from which a random sample of 98 cases was selected. Interviews were arranged with 41 respondents but ultimately achieved with 31 respondents. These interviews, undertaken by Linda Gilliland, a researcher employed by the SCSH, consisted of administration of a questionnaire yielding further quantitative data, followed by a taped semi-structured interview (Jones and Gilliland 1993; Jones and Stevens 1993). Fully transcribed qualitative data were available from 26 interviews and were analysed using The Ethnograph, a qualitative data analysis package (Seidel *et al.* 1988). The names used are pseudonyms.

Homeless Survey 1992

A sample of homeless young people in Scotland was achieved by the SCSH, through projects and agencies working with homeless people, housing and social work departments across Scotland, and other organizations likely to have contact with homeless young people. In all 138 organizations agreed to take part in the survey, which was conducted by the CES Survey Team. The aim was to obtain national coverage, and varied experience of homelessness.

The projects and agencies taking part were asked to administer a self-completion questionnaire to young people aged 16–22 who were presenting as homeless, who had attended secondary school in Scotland, and who

Figure A.2 Selection of 'risk' subset from SYPS 1987/89

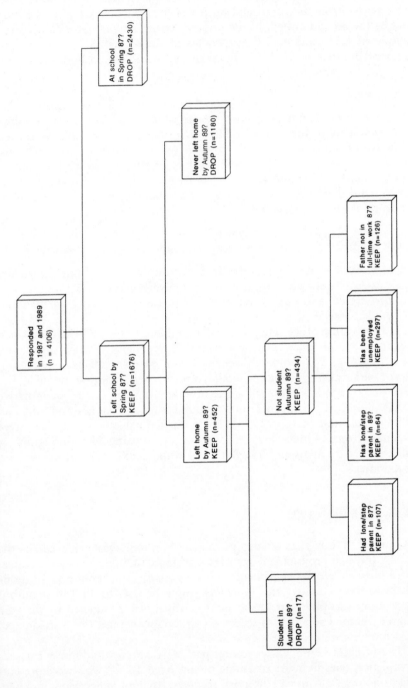

Young people in and out of the housing market

had not already taken part in the survey. The questionnaires were designed to allow comparison with data from the Scottish Young People's Surveys. Completed questionnaires were received from 183 people via 66 of the projects and agencies which had agreed to take part. In addition to the survey, personal interviews were undertaken with a further 63 homeless young people. The interview consisted of administration of the questionnaire, followed by semi-structured interview. For the quantitative analysis referred to in this book, the questionnaire data from interviews was combined with the Homeless Survey data, producing a total sample of 246 homeless young people across Scotland. Full details can be found in Jones and Stevens, 1993.

References

Abrams, P. (1961) *The Teenage Consumer*. London: London Press Exchange.
Ainley, P. (1991) *Young People Leaving Home*. London: Cassell.
Allan, G. and Crow, G. (eds) (1989) *Home and Family: Creating the Domestic Sphere*. Basingstoke: Macmillan.
Allatt, P. and Yeandle, S. (1986) 'It's not fair is it?' Youth unemployment, family relations and the social contract, in S. Allen *et al.* (eds) *The Experience of Unemployment*. London: Macmillan.
Allatt, P. and Yeandle, S. (1992) *Youth Unemployment and the Family: Voices of Disordered Times*. London: Routledge.
Allen, R. (1990) Punishing the parents. *Youth and Policy*, 31: 17–20.
Anderson, I. (1993) *Access to Housing for Low Income Single People: a Review of Research and Policy Issues*. York: Centre for Housing Policy, University of York.
Anderson, M. (1971) *Family Structure in Nineteenth Century Lancashire*. Cambridge: Cambridge University Press.
Anderson, M. (1983) What is new about the modern family: an historical perspective, in *The Family*, OPCS occasional paper no. 31. London: Office of Population Censuses and Surveys.
Baanders, A.N., Van Leeuwen, L.T. and Ploegmakers, M.J.H. (1989) *Uit huis gaan van jongeren. Een analyse van na-oorlogse veranderingen op basis van het Woningbehoefte-onderzoek 1985/6* [Youth leaving home. An analysis of changes after World War II on the basis of the Housing Demand Survey 1985/6]. Wageningen, Landbouw Universiteit.
Bates, I. and Riseborough, G. (1993) *Youth and Inequality*. Buckingham: Open University Press.
Bauer, G. and Cuzon, G. (1987) *Urban Environment Housing Solidarity: Consequences for Young People: the French Case*. Report for the European Foundation for the Improvement and Living and Working Conditions.
Beck, U. (1992) *Risk Society: Towards a New Modernity* (trans. M. Ritter). London: Sage.

Bell, C. (1968) *Middle Class Families: Social and Geographical Mobility*. London: Routledge.

Binns, D. and Mars, G. (1984) Family, community and unemployment: a study in change. *Sociological Review*, 32: 662–95.

Bloss, T., Frickey, A. and Godard, F. (1990) Cohabiter, décohabiter, recohabiter: itinéraires de générations de femmes. *Revue Française de Sociologie*, XXXI(4): 553–72.

Brannen, J., Dodd, K., Oakley, A. and Storey, P. (1994) *Young People, Health and Family Life*. Buckingham: Open University Press.

Brannen, K., Jones, G., Middleton, L. and Robertson, L. (1991) *Scottish Young People's Survey 1989 (Autumn): Technical Report*. Edinburgh: Centre for Educational Sociology.

Brannen, K. and Middleton, L. (1994) *Scottish Young People's Survey 1991 (Autumn): Technical Report*. Edinburgh: Centre for Educational Sociology.

Burton, P., Forrest, R. and Stewart, M. (1988) *Growing Up and Leaving Home*. An information booklet prepared for The European Foundation for the Improvement of Living and Working Conditions, Dublin.

Burton, P., Forrest, R. and Stewart, M. (1989) *Urban Environment, Accommodation, Social Cohesion: The Implications for Young People*, Consolidated report. Bristol: SAUS, University of Bristol.

Cheal, D. (1987) Intergenerational transfers and lifecourse management: towards a socio-economic perspective, in A. Bryman *et al.* (eds) *Rethinking the Life Cycle*. London: Macmillan.

Chisholm, L. and Bergeret, J-M. (1991) *Young people in the European Community: Towards an Agenda for Research and Policy*. Report prepared on behalf of the Commission of the European Communities Task Force 'Human Resources, Education, Training and Youth', Commission of the European Economic Communities.

Clarke, E. (1989) *Young Single Mothers Today: A Qualitative Study of Housing Needs*. National Council for Single Parents.

Cohen, S. (1973) *Folk Devils and Moral Panics*. St Albans: Paladin.

Coleman, J.S. (1961) *The Adolescent Society*. New York: Free Press.

Coles, B. (1995, forthcoming) *Youth, Citizenship and Social Policy*. London: UCL Press.

Commission of the European Communities (1982) *The Young Europeans: An Explanatory Study of 15–24 year olds in EEC Countries*. Brussels: DG Information.

Commission of the European Communities (1989) *Young Europeans in 1987*. Luxembourg: Office for Official Publications of the European Communities.

Commission of the European Communities (1991) *Les Jeunes Europeens en 1990*. Brussels: Task Force Human Resources, Education, Training and Youth, June (Draft)

Crook, J. and Dalgleish, M. (1994) Homeless young people into jobs and homes – a study of the Foyer pilots. *Employment Gazette*, March, 77–81.

Crow, G. (1989a) The post-war development of the modern domestic ideal, in G. Allan and G. Crow (eds) *Home and Family: Creating the Domestic Sphere*. London: Macmillan.

Crow, G. (1989b) The use of the concept of 'strategy' in recent sociological literature. *Sociology*, 23(1): 1–24.

Crowther, M.A. (1982) Family responsibility and state responsibility in Britain before the Welfare State. *Historical Journal*, 25(1): 131–45.

Cusack, S. and Roll, J. (1985) *Families Rent Apart*. London: Child Poverty Action Group.

Davies, B. (1986) *Threatening Youth: Towards a National Youth Policy*. Milton Keynes: Open University Press.

De Jong Gierveld, J., Liefbroer, A.C. and Beekink, E. (1991) The effect of parental resources on patterns of leaving home among young adults in the Netherlands. *European Sociological Review*, 7(1): 55–71.

Deacon, A. and Bradshaw, J. (1983) *Reserved for the Poor*. Oxford: Blackwell.

Deelstra, T. and Schokkenbroek, J. (1988) *Housing for Young People in the Netherlands*. Report for the European Foundation for the Improvement of Living and Working Conditions.

Deem, R. (1985) Leisure, work and unemployment: old traditions and new boundaries, in R. Deem and G. Salaman (eds) *Work, Culture and Society*. Milton Keynes: Open University Press.

Dennis, N. and Erdos, G. (1992) *Families without Fatherhood*, Choice in Welfare Series no 12. London: IEA Health and Welfare Unit.

Department of the Environment (1981) *Single and Homeless*. London: HMSO.

Department of the Environment (1993) Survey of single homeless people. *In Brief*, Housing Research Summary no. 5.

Dunnell, K. (1979) *Family Formation Survey, 1976*. London: HMSO.

Emmanuel, D. (1987) *Housing Problems of Young People in Urban Areas: The Case of Greece*. Report for the European Foundation for the Improvement of Living and Working Conditions.

Employment Department (1993, undated) *No Job, No Money, No Home . . . No Job: How to Break this Vicious Circle*, summary of a study by Policy Studies Institute, Employment Department.

Ermisch, J. and Overton, E. (1984) *Minimal Household Units: A New Perspective on the Demographic and Economic Analysis of Household Formation*. London: Policy Studies Institute.

Finch, J. (1989a) *Family Obligations and Social Change*. Cambridge: Polity Press.

Finch, J. (1989b) Policy assumptions about family support and their implications for social security. Paper presented at the International Seminar on *The Sociology of Social Security*, Edinburgh, July.

Finch, J. and Mason, J. (1993) *Negotiating Family Responsibilities*. London: Routledge.

Forrest, R. and Kennett, T. (1994) Coping strategies among households with negative equity. Paper presented to the ISA XIIIth World Congress, Bielefeld, Germany, July.

Forrest, R. and Murie, A. (1994) Residential mobility, housing exclusion and social stratification in Britain: some research evidence. Paper presented to the ISA XIIIth World Congress, Bielefeld, Germany, July.

Furlong, A. and Cooney, G. (1990) Getting on their bikes: teenagers leaving home in Scotland in the 1980s. *Journal of Social Policy*, 19(4): 535–51.

Galland, O. (1990) Un nouvel age de la vie. *Revue Française de Sociologie*, XXXI-4: 529–51.

Gibbs, I. and Kemp, P.A. (1993) Housing Benefit and income redistribution. *Urban Studies*, 30(1): 63–72.

Giddens, A. (1991) *Modernity and Self-Identity: Self and Society in the Late Modern Age*. Cambridge: Polity Press.

Giddens, A. (1994) Modernity and the question of tradition. Paper presented at the symposium. *Tradition, Modernity and Post-Modernity*, International Socio-logical Association XIIIth World Congress, Bielefeld, Germany, July.

Gillis, J.R. (1985) *For Better or Worse: British Marriage 1600 to the Present.* Oxford: Oxford University Press.

Gilman, C.P. (1980) The home: its work and influence, in E. Malos (ed.) *The Politics of Housework.* London: Allison and Busby.

Godard, F. and Bloss, T. (1988) La décohabitation des jeunes, in C. Bonvalet and P. Merlin (eds) *Transformation de la Famille et Habitat, Actes du Colloque,* 31–35, Paris: Presses Universitaires de France.

Goldscheider, F.K. and LeBourdais, C. (1986) The decline in age at leaving home. *Sociology and Social Research*, 70: 143–5.

Goode, W. (1982) *The Family*, 2nd edn. Englewood Cliffs, New Jersey: Prentice-Hall Inc.

Graham, H. (1983) Caring: a labour of love, in J. Finch and D. Groves (eds) *A Labour of Love: Women, Work and Caring.* London: Routledge and Kegan Paul.

Greve, J. (with Currie, E.) (1991) *Homelessness in Britain.* York: Joseph Rowntree Foundation

Halsey, A.H. (1992) Introduction, in N. Dennis and G. Erdos, *Families without Fatherhood.* London: IEA Health and Welfare Unit.

Hardey, M. and Crow, G. (eds) (1991) *Lone Parenthood: Coping with Constraints and Making Opportunities.* Hemel Hempstead: Harvester Wheatsheaf.

Harris, C. (1983) *The Family and Industrial Society.* London: Allen and Unwin.

Harris, N. (1989) *Social Security for Young People.* Aldershot: Avebury.

Haskey, J. (1983) Social class patterns of marriage. *Population Trends*, 34: 12–19.

Haskey, J. (1984) Social class and socio-economic differences in divorce in England and Wales. *Population Studies*, 38(3): 419–49.

Haywood, I. (1984) Housing in Denmark, in M. Wynn (ed.) *Housing in Europe.* London: Croom Helm.

Heer, D.M., Hodge, R.W. and Felson, M. (1984/5) The cluttered nest. Evidence that young adults are more likely to live at home than in the recent past. *Sociology and Social Research*, 69: 436–41.

Hendessi, M. (1992) Support for young women homeless because of sexual abuse. *Findings*, 54. York: Joseph Rowntree Foundation.

Hudson, F. and Ineichen, B. (1991) *Taking it Lying Down: Sexuality and Teenage Motherhood.* Basingstoke: Macmillan.

Hutson, S. and Jenkins, R. (1989) *Taking the Strain: Families, Unemployment and the Transition to Adulthood.* Milton Keynes: Open University Press.

Hutson, S. and Liddiard, M. (1991) *Young and Homeless in Wales: Government Policies, Insecure Accommodation and Agency Support.* Swansea: Department of Sociology and Anthropology, University College, Swansea.

Hutson, S. and Liddiard, M. (1994) *Youth Homelessness: The Construction of a Social Issue.* Basingstoke: Macmillan.

Ineichen, B. (1981) The housing decisions of young people. *British Journal of Sociology*, 32(2): 252–8.

Jamieson, L. and Corr, H. (1990) *'Earning your Keep': Self Reliance and Family Obligation*, Economic and Social Research Council 16019 Initiative occasional papers no. 30, SSRU, City University.

Jablonka, P., Potter, P. and Unterseher, L. (1987) *Urban Environment, Accommodation and Social Cohesion: The Implications for Young People.* Report for the European Foundation for the Improvement of Living and Working Conditions.

Johnson, B., Murie, A., Naumann, L. and Yanetta, A. (1991) *A Typology of Homelessness*, discussion paper no. 3. Edinburgh: Scottish Homes.

Jones, G. (1987a) Leaving the parental home: an analysis of early housing careers. *Journal of Social Policy*, 16(1): 49–74.

Jones, G. (1987b) Young workers in the class structure. *Work, Employment and Society*, 1(4): 487–508.

Jones, G. (1988) Integrating process and structure in the concept of youth. *Sociological Review*, 36(4): 706–31.

Jones, G. (1990) *Household Formation among Young Adults in Scotland*. Edinburgh: Scottish Homes.

Jones, G. (1991) The cost of living in the parental home. *Youth and Policy*, 32: 19–29.

Jones, G. (1992a) Leaving home in rural Scotland. *Youth and Policy*, 39: 34–44.

Jones, G. (1992b) Short-term reciprocity in parent-child economic exchanges, in C. Marsh and S. Arber (eds) *Household and Family: Divisions and Change*, Basingstoke: Macmillan.

Jones, G. (1993a) *The Process of Leaving Home: Regulated Entry into the Housing Market?*, working paper no. 2, Young people in and out of the housing market research project, Centre for Educational Sociology, University of Edinburgh and Scottish Council for Single Homeless.

Jones, G. (1993b) *On the Margins of the Housing Market: Housing and Homelessness in Youth*, working paper no. 3, Young people in and out of the housing market research project, Centre for Educational Sociology, University of Edinburgh and Scottish Council for Single Homeless.

Jones, G. (1995) *Family Support for Young People*. London: Family Policy Studies Centre.

Jones, G. and Gilliland, L. (1993) *'I Would Hate to be Young Again': Biographies of Risk and its Avoidance*, working paper no. 4, Young people in and out of the housing market research project, Centre for Educational Sociology, University of Edinburgh and Scottish Council for Single Homeless.

Jones, G. and Stevens, C. (1993) *Researching 'Young People In and Out of the Housing Market': about the Project*, working paper no. 5, Young people in and out of the housing market research project, Centre for Educational Sociology, University of Edinburgh and Scottish Council for Single Homeless.

Jones, G. and Wallace, C. (1990) Beyond individualization: What sort of social change?, in L. Chisholm *et al.* (eds) *Childhood, Youth and Social Change: A Comparative Perspective*. London: Falmer Press.

Jones, G. and Wallace, C. (1992) *Youth, Family and Citizenship*, Buckingham: Open University Press.

Joseph Rowntree Foundation (1991) Grand entrance for foyers. *Innovations in Social Housing*, 1, October.

Joseph Rowntree Foundation (1994a) Self-build schemes for homeless young people. *Findings*, Housing Research 116, June.

Joseph Rowntree Foundation (1994b) Housing association lettings to homeless people. *Findings*, Housing Research 117, July.

Kearns, A. (1992) Affordability for housing association tenants: a key issue for British social housing policy. *Journal of Social Policy*, 21(4): 525–49.

Keilman, N. (1987) Recent trends in family and household composition in Europe. *European Journal of Population*, 3: 291–325.

Kemp, P., Oldman, C., Rugg, J. and Williams, T. (1994) *The Effects of Benefit on Housing Decisions*, Department of Social Security research report no. 26. London: HMSO.

Kennedy, L.W. and Stokes, D.W. (1982) Extended family support and the high cost of housing. *Journal of Marriage and the Family*, 44: 311–18.

Kiernan, K. (1983) The structure of families today: continuity or change?, in *The Family*, OPCS occasional paper no. 31. London: Office of Population Censuses and Surveys.

Kiernan, K. (1985) *A Demographic Analysis of First Marriages in England and Wales: 1950–1985*, CPS research paper 85–1. London: Centre for Population Studies.

Kiernan, K. (1986) Leaving home: a comparative analysis of six Western European countries. *European Journal of Population*, 2(2): 177–84.

Kiernan, K. (1992) The impact of family disruption in childhood on transitions made in young adult life. *Population Studies*, 46(2): 213–34.

Kiernan, K. and Wicks, M. (1990) *Family Change and Future Policy*. London: Family Policy Studies Centre (with Joseph Rowntree Foundation)

Kearns, A. (1992) Affordability for housing association tenants: a key issue for British social housing policy. *Journal of Social Policy*, 21(4): 525–49.

Kirk, D., Nelson, S., Sinfield, A and Sinfield, D. (1991) *Excluding Youth: Poverty Among Young People Living Away from Home*. Edinburgh: Centre for Social Welfare Research, University of Edinburgh.

Laslett, P. (1971) *The World We Have Lost*. London: Methuen.

Leonard, D. (1980) *Sex and Generation: A Study of Courtship and Weddings*. London: Tavistock.

Leridon, H. and Villeneuve-Gokalp, C. (1988) Les nouvaux couples. Nombres caractéristiques et attitudes. *Population*, 43: 331–74.

Liddiard, M. and Hutson, S. (1991a) Youth Homelessness in Wales, in C. Wallace and M. Cross (eds) *Youth in Transition: The Sociology of Youth and Youth Policy*. London: Falmer Press.

Liddiard, M. and Hutson, S. (1991b) Homeless young people and runaways – agency definitions and processes. *Journal of Social Policy*, 20(3): 365–88.

Lister, R. (1990) Women, economic dependency and citizenship. *Journal of Social Policy*, 19(4): 445–67.

Maas, F. (1986) Family conflict and leaving home. *Bulletin of the National Clearinghouse for Youth Studies*, 5(1): 9–13.

MacDonald, R. (1988) Out of town, out of work: research on the post-16 experience in two rural areas, in B. Coles (ed.) *Young Careers*. Milton Keynes: Open University Press.

McKee, L. (1987) Households during unemployment: the resourcefulness of the unemployed, in J. Brannen and G. Wilson (eds) *Give and Take in Families: Studies in Resource Distribution*. London: Allen and Unwin.

Maclagan, I. (1992) *A Broken Promise: The Failure of the Youth Training Policy*. Published by Youthaid and the Children's Society, on behalf of the Coalition On Young People and Social Security (COYPSS).

McLaverty, P. and Kemp, P. (1994) Social exclusion and claimant strategies. Paper presented at the International Sociological Association XIIIth World Congress, Bielefeld, Germany, July.

McLennan, D. (1994) *A Competitive UK Economy: The Challenges for Housing Policy*. York: Joseph Rowntree Foundation.

MacLennan, E., Fitz, J. and Sullivan, J. (1985) *Working Children*, pamphlet no. 34. London: Low Pay Unit.

Mansfield, P. and Collard, J. (1988) *The Beginning of the Rest of your Life? A Portrait of Newly-Wed Marriage*. Basingstoke: Macmillan.

Marsland, D. (1986) Young people, the family and the state, in D. Anderson and G. Dawson (eds) *Family Portraits*. London: Social Affairs Unit.

Mayer, K.U. and Schwarz, K. (1989) The process of leaving the parental home: some German data, in E. Grebenik, C. Hohn and R. Mackensen (eds) *Later Phases of the Family Cycle*. Oxford: Clarendon Press.

Modell, J. and Hareven, T.K. (1973) Urbanisation and the malleable household: boarding and lodging in American families. *Journal of Marriage and the Family*, 35: 467–79.

Moore, B. (1984) *Privacy: Studies in Social and Cultural History*. New York: Sharpe.

Morgan-Klein, B. (1985) *Where Am I Going to Stay? A Report on Young People Leaving Care in Scotland*. Edinburgh: Scottish Council for Single Homeless.

MORI (1991) *A Survey of 16 and 17 year old Applicants for Severe Hardship Payments*. Research study conducted for Department of Social Security, July.

Munro, M. and Smith, S.J. (1989) Gender and housing: broadening the debate. *Housing Studies*, 4: 3–17.

Murphy, M.J. and Sullivan, O. (1983) *Housing tenure and fertility in post-war Britain*. CPS research paper 83–2. London: Centre for Population Studies, London School of Hygiene and Tropical Medicine.

Murray, C. (1990) *The Emerging British Underclass*. London: IEA Health and Welfare Unit.

Nicholson, L. and Wasoff, F. (1989) *Student Experience of Private Rented Housing in Edinburgh*. Edinburgh: Department of Social Policy and Social Work, Student Accommodation Service, University of Edinburgh.

O'Carroll, A. (1992) *Young Single Parents: Access to Housing in Edinburgh*, research paper no. 38. Edinburgh: School of Planning and Housing, Edinburgh College of Art/Heriot-Watt University.

Oakley, A. (1976) *Housewife*. Harmondsworth: Penguin.

Office of Population Censuses and Surveys (1993) *General Household Survey 1991*, GHS no. 22. London: HMSO.

Parsons, T. (1956) *Family: Socialization and Interaction Processes*. London: Routledge and Kegan Paul.

Pateman, C. (1989) *The Disorder of Women*. Cambridge: Polity/Basil Blackwell.

Peelo, M., Stewart, G., Prior, A. and Stewart, J. (1990) A sense of grievance: homelessness, poverty and youth offenders. *Youth Social Work*, 2: 12–13.

Penhale, B. (1990) *Living Arrangements of Young Adults in France and England and Wales*, LS working paper no. 68. London: Social Statistics Research Unit, City University.

Phoenix, A. (1991) *Young Mothers?* Cambridge: Polity Press.

Pickvance, C. and Pickvance, K. (1994a) Towards a strategic approach to housing behaviour: a study of young people's housing strategies in South-East England. *Sociology*, 28(3): 657–77.

Pickvance, C. and Pickvance, K. (1994b) The role of family help in the housing decisions of young people. *Sociological Review*, forthcoming.

Randall, G. (1988) *No Way Home: Homeless Young People in London*. London: Centrepoint.
Rauta, I. (1986) *Who would prefer separate accommodation?* OPCS, Social Survey Division. London: HMSO.
Rhodes, D. (1993) The state of the private rented sector. *Findings*, 90. York: Joseph Rowntree Foundation.
Roll, J. (1990) *Young People: Growing Up in the Welfare State*. London: Family Policy Studies Centre.
Roll, J. (1993) *Lone Parent Families in the European Commission*. London: Family Policy Studies Centre.
Rural Development Commission (1992) *Homelessness in Rural Areas*. Salisbury: Rural Development Commission.
Schnaiberg, A. and Goldenberg, A. (1989) From empty nest to crowded nest. The dynamics of incompletely-launched young adults. *Social Problems*, 36: 251–69.
Schwarz, K. (1983) Les menages en Republique Federale d'Allemagne: 1961–1972–1981. *Population*, 38(3).
Seidel, J.V., Kjolseth, R. and Seymour, E. (1988) *The Ethnograph*. Amherst, MA: Qualis Research Associates.
Sharp, C. (1991) Homelessness, housing benefit and the private rented sector. *Findings*, 28. York: Joseph Rowntree Foundation.
Shelter (1991) *Living on the Borderline: Homeless Young Scots in London*. Report by Shelter, Borderline and Centrepoint Soho. London: Shelter.
Shepherd, P. (1985) *The National Child Development Study: an Introduction to the Background of the Study and the Methods of Data Collection*, working paper no. 1. London: NCDS User Support Group, Social Statistics Research Unit, City University.
Siltanen, J. (1986) Domestic responsibilities and the structuring of employment, in R. Crompton and M. Mann (eds) *Gender and Stratification*. Cambridge: Polity Press.
Siltanen, J. (1995) *Locating Gender – Occupational Segregation, Wages and Domestic Responsibilities*. London: UCL Press.
Smith, J. and Gilford, S. (1991) Homelessness among under-25s. *Findings*, 48. York: Joseph Rowntree Foundation.
SSAC (1984) *The Draft Housing Benefits Amendment Regulations 1984, and the Supplementary Benefits (Requirements) Amendment Regulations 1984*. Reports of the Social Security Advisory Committee in accordance with Section 10(3) of the Social Security Act 1990, February 1984. Cmnd 9150 (SSAC Report), para28.
Somerville, P. (1992) Homelessness and the meaning of home: rooflessness or rootlessness? *International Journal of Urban and Regional Research*, 16(4): 529–39.
Steger, A. (1979) Ubergange zwischen privaten Haushalten: eine mikroanalytische Untersuchung, Frankfurt/Mannheim. (Quoted in Mayer and Schwarz, op cit.)
Stein, M. and Carey, K. (1986) *Leaving Care*. Oxford: Blackwell.
Stockley, D., Bishopp, D. and Cantor, D. (1993) *Young People on the Move*. Department of Psychology, University of Surrey.
Strathclyde Poverty Alliance (1992) *Youth Destitution in Strathclyde*. Glasgow: Strathclyde Poverty Alliance.
Study Group on Homelessness (1994) *Homelessness*, 1991/92 Co-ordinated Research

Programme in the Social Field, Steering Committee on Social Policy. Strasbourg: Council of Europe Press.

Sullivan O. and Murphy, M. (1984) Housing pathways and stratification: some evidence from a British national survey. *Journal of Social Policy*, 13: 147–65.

Thatcher, M. (1987) Interview with Douglas Keay, *Woman's Own*, 31 October.

Thornton, R. (1990) *The New Homeless*. London: Sheltered Housing Aid Centre.

Turner, B. (1993) Outline of a theory of human rights. *Sociology*, 27(3): 489–512.

van Vliet, W. (1988) The housing and living arrangements of young people in the United States, in E. Hutman and W. van Vliet (eds) *Handbook of Housing and the Built Environment in the United States*. New York: Greenwood Press.

Walker, R. (1988) The costs of household formation, in R. Walker and G. Parker (eds) *Money Matters: Income, Wealth and Financial Welfare*. London: Sage.

Wall, R. (1978) The age at leaving home. *Journal of Family History*, 3(2): 181–202.

Wall, R (1987) Leaving home and the process of household formation in pre-industrial England. *Continuity and Change*, 2(1): 77–101.

Wallace, C. (1987) *For Richer, For Poorer: Growing Up In and Out of Work*. London: Tavistock.

Wallace, C. (1991) Young people in rural south-west England. *Youth and Policy*, 25: 35–6.

Watson, S. and Austerberry, H. (1986) *Housing and Homelessness: A Feminist Perspective*. London: Routledge and Kegan Paul.

Wicks, M. (1991) Social politics 1979–1992: families, work and welfare. Paper presented to the Social Policy Association Annual Conference, Nottingham, July.

Williams, B. (1992) *Making a Start: Young People and Housing Associations*. London: National Federation of Housing Associations and Young Homelessness Group.

Willis, P. (1984) Youth unemployment, *New Society*, 29 March, 5 April and 12 April.

Young, C.M. (1974) Ages, reasons and sex differences for children leaving home: observations from survey data in Australia. *Journal of Marriage and the Family*, November, 769–78.

Young, C.M. (1984) Leaving home and returning home: a demographic study of young adults in Australia. Australian Family Research Conference Proceedings, Canberra, vol. 1: Family Formation, Structure, Values, 53–76.

Young, C.M. (1987) *Young People Leaving Home in Australia: The Trend Towards Independence*, Australian Family Formation Project monograph no. 9. Canberra.

Index

social class
  and change, 10
  and early leaving, 47
  and family support, 146–8, 149
  and housing, 106–7, 113
  and leaving home, 22, 26–7
  and returning home, 63, 65
  solidarities, 7, 8
Social Fund loans, 11, 81
social housing, 14, 105–6, 114
  and pregnancy, 32, 55, 108
social justice, and rights claims, 20
social legitimacy
  assumptions of, 32–4, 42, 146–8, 149
  cross-national variations, 28
  leavers' perceptions, 54–8
  and support, 32–4, 38, 39, 145
  and tradition, 19–27, 39, 82–3
social relations, 3
Social Security Advisory Committee
  (SSAC), 83
social self-build projects, 154
social structure, limitations, 5–6
Somerville, P., 3
Spain, 33
state support/benefits, 93–4
  withdrawal, 8, 10, 11–12, 30, 33, 43,
    44, 46–7, 61, 66, 80–1, 99, 146–8,
    153, 154
Steger, A., 32
step-parents
  and early leaving, 47–8, 49–50
  and homelessness, 50
  and support, 86
stereotyping, 6, 7
Stewart, G., 78
Stewart, J., 78
Stewart, M., 20, 28, 29, 32, 33, 35, 69,
  90, 104, 116
Stockley, D., 50, 78
Stokes, D.W., 83
Storey, P., 72
strategy
  coping, 126
  housing, 102, 107–8, 109, 114–17,
    126–7, 140–1, 144
  survival, 8, 53, 143
Strathclyde Poverty Alliance, 100
student loans, 10
students, *see* education
Sullivan, J., 83
Sullivan, O., 113
support, *see also* family support;
  financial support; state support
supported accommodation, 141

supported independence, 91, 94–5
supported returners, 91–2
surrogate households, 3, 27, 64, 108–9
survival strategy, and risk avoidance/
  reduction, 8, 53, 143

taxpayers, rights, 11
teenage leavers, analysis, 47–9
temporary accommodation, 141
tenancy agreements, 12
Thatcher, M., 5–6
theft, 100
Thornton, R., 50
timing, and choice, 28, 39, 44–6,
  145–6, 148
tradition, and social legitimacy, 19–27,
  39, 82–3
traditional family values, 6, 7, 82–3
training/training schemes, 10–11, 37
  and homelessness, 118
  housing costs, not covered by
    allowances, 10, 12, 30, 71, 80
  income link, 152
  as leaving home reason, 43, 44
  unemployment consequence, 30
transitional housing, 27, 104–5, 108
transitions
  affected by unemployment, 30
  child to parent, 21
  dependence to citizenship, 21, 28
  education to work, 21
  extended, 23–5
  normative condensed, 22–3
  parental to partnership/independant
    home, 21, 28–9, 145
  patterns, 36–7, 144–6
  protracted, 21–2
trust, and risk-taking, 127
Turner, B., 20

underclass, 5, 61, 143–4, 149
unemployment, 30, 34
  in family, 43, 51, 144
  homelessness cycle, 118, 124, 154
  and negativity of home, 3
Unemployment Benefit, 11, 80
United States of America, 34
unsupported independence, 91, 93–4
unsupported returners, 91, 92–3
Unterseher, L., 32, 35
urban areas, difference from rural, 22

values, traditional, 6, 7, 82–3
Van Leeuwen, L.T., 31
Villeneuve-Gokalp, C., 34

YOUTH, FAMILY AND CITIZENSHIP
Gill Jones and Claire Wallace

This important text examines how young people growing up come to be recognized as independent citizens and to what extent access to citizenship is determined by their economic circumstances and level of economic dependency. It explores how the transition from dependent child to independent adult is structured by relationships with family members, the market place and the institutions of the state. It considers how much freedom young people really have to make decisions about their lives, and identifies inequalities of opportunity and choice, stemming from their social class, gender, ethnicity, location and economic status. The text integrates often separated aspects of young people's lives – as family and peer group members, as trainees or workers, and as consumers.

This is essential reading for students and researchers across the social sciences, especially those concerned with social policy, youth and community work, sociology and education.

Contents
Youth, family and citizenship – Structuring economic dependency – Social citizenship by proxy? – Dependence on their families? – Independence from their families? – Consumer citizens? – Rethinking youth and citizenship – Appendix – References – Indexes.

192pp   0 335 09294 2 (Paperback)   0 335 09299 3 (Hardback)

YOUTH AND INEQUALITY

Inge Bates and George Riseborough

This book consists of a unique and fascinating collection of qualitative and ethnographic studies of differing groups of young people. It examines inequality in all its complexity in the lived experience of youth and shows the continued pervasive influence of class and gender. The groups studied range from young women in private education to youth training 'lads' and gives vivid and insightful accounts of their social existence. Their diverse experiences are explored in the context of family, education, training, work and politics. The contributors consider for example, family and educational processes, social divisions and control, identities and opportunities, 'enterprise' careers and cultural resistance in the context of late/post modern transitions. *Youth and Inequality* is essential reading for students and researchers in the social sciences, education and cultural studies and will be of interest to all those professionally engaged with young people.

Contents
Introduction: Deepening divisions, fading solutions – A job which is 'right for me'?: Social class, gender and individualization – Learning a living or living a learning?: An ethnography of BTEC National Diploma students – 'When I have my own studio . . .': The making and shaping of 'designer' careers – Running, plodding, falling: The practice and politics of youth enterprise – A yuppie generation?: Political and cultural options for A-level students – Gaining the edge: Girls at a private school – Becoming privileged: The role of family processes – 'GBH – The Gobbo Barmy Harmy': One day in the life of 'the YTS boys' – Career trajectories and the mirage of increased social mobility – Index.

272pp   0 335 15695 9 (Paperback)